# CONTENTS

KV-621-511

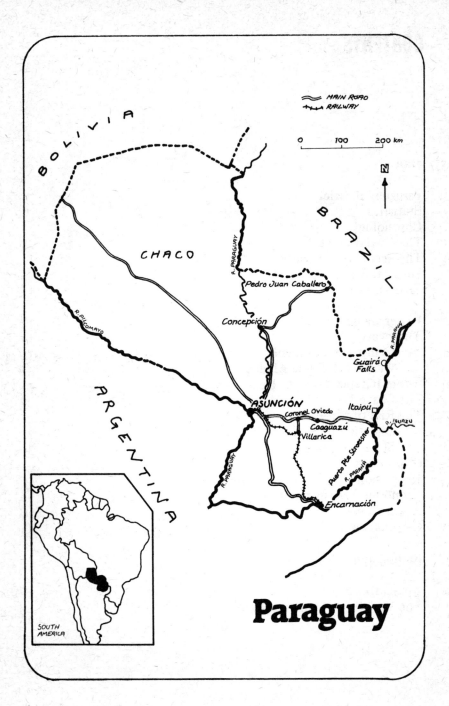

MAIN ROAD
RAILWAY

0    100    200 km

N

BOLIVIA

BRAZIL

CHACO

R. PARAGUAY

Pedro Juan Caballero

Concepción

R. PILOMAYO

Guairá
Falls

R. PARANÁ

ARGENTINA

ASUNCIÓN

Coronel Oviedo

Itaipú

R. IGUAZU

Caaguazú
Villarica

R. PARAGUAY

Puerto Pte Strossner

R. PARANÁ

Encarnación

SOUTH
AMERICA

# Paraguay

QMC          723435 7

a30213 007234357b

# PARAGUAY
# Power Game

DATE DUE FOR RETURN

**Latin America Bureau**
**Research and Action on Latin America**

First published in Great Britain in 1980 by

Latin American Bureau (Research and Action) Ltd
PO Box 134
London NW1 4JY

Copyright © Latin America Bureau (Research and Action) Ltd, 1980
ISBN 0 906156 10 6

A Bolivar Design
Maps by Splendid Designing
Typeset, printed and bound by the Russell Press Ltd,
Nottingham

# PARAGUAY IN BRIEF

## Statistics

| | | |
|---|---|---|
| **Area** | 157,000 sq. miles (UK = 94,200 sq. miles) | |
| **Population (1979)** | Total | 2,973,000 |
| | Growth | 3.3% (annual average rate 1970-79) |
| | Urban | 36% |
| **The People** | Race | Largely *mestizo* (mixed blood); indigenous peoples — 100,000 |
| | Language | Guaraní and Spanish |
| | Religion | Roman Catholic |
| **Economy (1979)** | GDP | Total US$2,106 million Per capita US$708 |
| | Trade | Exports US$370 million Imports US$570 million |
| | Principal exports: | cotton (33%); vegetable oils inc. soya bean (27%); wood (14%); meat products (4%); tobacco (3%) |
| | Main markets: | Argentina, West Germany, Holland, Brazil |

| | 1970-74 (av.) | 1975 | 1976 | 1977 | 1978 | 1979 |
|---|---|---|---|---|---|---|
| GDP Growth (%) | 6.4 | 5.0 | 7.5 | 11.8 | 10.0 | 9.5 |

Inflation  Official 26%
Unofficial 62%

| Income | | Share of national income (1973) | | |
|---|---|---|---|---|
| Distribution | Top 2% | Top 28% | Middle 42% | Bottom 30% |
| | 14% | 66% | 30% | 4% |

Rural
incomes:  80% of all farms are less than 50 acres;
(1978)  averages per capita income US$137

Health  Life expectancy at birth: 63 years
(1977)  Infant mortality: 95.2 per thousand live births
One doctor per 1,190 people
Access to safe water: 7% of population

*Sources:* Central Bank; Flecha, *Distribución de Ingreso y Sub-desarrollo*, Asunción 1975; Inter-American Development Bank; *Paraguay Económico*; World Bank.

Note: Reliable statistics are particularly difficult to obtain in Paraguay and official figures should be treated with scepticism. For example, international organizations, such as the World Bank, estimate imports at least 45% higher and exports about 60% higher than official figures, due to smuggling (see page 54).

# Chronology

1537   Foundation of Asunción by Spanish.

1811   Independence from Spain.

1814-65   Nationalist governments of Dr Rodrigues de Francia and Carlos Antonio López.

1865-70   War of the Triple Alliance against Argentina, Brazil and Uruguay.

1932-35   Chaco War against Bolivia.

1936   Febrerista coup by war veterans.

1940-46   Pro-Axis military dictatorship of General Higinio Morinigo.

1946   Nine-month period of political freedom allowing expression of growing social discontent.

1947   Colorado Party defeats combined forces of opposition in civil war.

1954   General Alfredo Stroessner takes power in 4 May coup.

1956   Introduction of IMF stabilization programme.

1958   General strike crushed and trade union movement intervened.

1959   Stroessner closes parliament and purges *civilista* wing of Colorado Party, who flee into exile where they set up MOPOCO in opposition to Stroessner.

1959-60   Guerilla invasions by *Movimiento 14 de Mayo* and FULNA are wiped out by armed forces.

1966   Brazilian troops occupy disputed border area around Guairá Falls.

1969   Anti-US student demonstrations during visit of Nelson Rockefeller; excommunication of Interior Minister and Chief of Police following invasion of church property.

1972   Stroessner finally extradites Mafia heroin boss Augeste Ricord following threatened withdrawal of US support.

1973    Stroessner signs controversial Itaipú treaty with Brazil.

1974    Hundreds arrested and several deaths in police custody following abortive plot to blow up Stroessner with van loaded with dynamite.

1975    Anti-guerilla troops destroy peasant cooperative at Jejui, shooting peasants and arresting all 300 inhabitants (February), followed by nation-wide attacks on *ligas agarias* movement; arrest of 150 accused of Communist Party membership; arrest and death under torture of Dr Miguel Angel Soler, head of Communist Party and two other members of central committee (December).

1976    Security forces smash embryonic armed resistance movement, First of March Organization (OPM); 2,000 peasants and 200 students arrested with 20 deaths in police custody (April/May).

1977    Dr Agustin Goiburú, leader of MOPOCO, kidnapped in Argentina by Paraguayan police and disappears (February); arrest and trial of 17 activists of student-based Independent Movement who planned campaign for renegotiation of Itaipú Treaty (July); arrest of 19 trade union and peasant leaders (December).

1978    Stroessner 're-elected' for further five years with 89.6% of vote in election excluding almost all of the legal opposition; Organisation of American States condemns human rights violations in Paraguay (June); opposition leader Domingo Laino denounces Stroessner in US Congress and is kidnapped on return to Asunción; Stroessner forced to release Laino following international protest; peasant leader Doroteo Brandel killed weeks after his release from two years secret imprisonment (August); 400 attend first national human rights congress in Asunción (December).

1979    National Accord (AN) signed by four opposition parties (February); World Anti-Communist League holds biannual congress in Asunción (April); deposed dictator of Nicaragua, Anastasio Somoza, granted refuge in Paraguay (August); opposition leader Domingo Laino re-arrested (September); arrest of journalist's union leader González Delvalle (November); Domingo Laino released (December).

**1980**  Council of delegates of Paraguayan Confederation of
Workers (CPT) meets for first time in 20 years (February);
20 peasants killed and over 200 arrested following protest
against land evictions in Caaguazú (March); release of
Virgilio Bareiro, political prisoner detained without trial
since 1964 (May).

# The Government

### The Formal Structure

An official publication of the Paraguayan embassy in Britain,
designed to attract foreign investment, describes the country's
political institutions as follows:

'Paraguay is a unitary and representative Republic, ruled by a
Constitution which provides for separate Executive, Legislative
and Judiciary Powers.

The President of the Republic is the head of the Executive,
elected by direct vote for a term of five years, and with the right
to be re-elected. The President is assisted by a Cabinet of 11
Ministers, members of the Executive.

The Legislative Power consists of a Parliament with two Houses,
the House of Representatives and the Senate. Both Houses are
elected by direct vote for a 5-year period.

The Judiciary is exercised by a 5-member Supreme Court of
Justice, appointed by the Executive, the Courts of Appeal and
the Magistrate Courts'.

This formal description however fails to reveal the extreme
concentration of power in the hands of Stroessner and a handful
of trusted military and civilian colleagues, who have become
millionaires from the fruits of the rampant corruption which
characterizes the regime.

### The Executive

In 1978 Stroessner was re-elected President for a sixth consecutive
term of office (1978-83). In order to do this, a constituent
assembly in 1977 amended the 1967 constituiton which
permitted only one period of re-election. Elections in Paraguay are
blatantly fraudulent. In the 1978 presidential election several large
towns registered not a single vote for the opposition. The govern-

ment exercises a complete monopoly over the mass media at election times and only pro-Stroessner posters are displayed in public places.

## The Legislature

The maintenance of a facade of parliamentary democracy has been a permanent feature of Stroessner's rule. The bulk of the opposition has been denied parliamentary representation through non-recognition by the electoral board, but the token electoral opposition is assured of one-third of all seats in parliament, whatever their share of the total vote case. The legislature is subservient to the dictates of Stroessner, and has never rejected a proposed bill emanating from the executive.

## The Judiciary

The rule of law does not exist in Paraguay. There is no independence of the judiciary. Although expressly forbidden by the constitution, all Supreme Court judges must be members of the Colorado Party and must obey Stroessner's orders. The mere accusation by the police that a person has been guilty of some illegal act is sufficient to ensure conviction. It is not necessary to offer evidence nor summon witness.

## The State of Siege

Stroessner has maintained a state of siege constantly since 1954, lifting it on only six occasions, on five of them for a mere 24 hours, to coincide with elections. The justification for the state of siege is the threat of 'communist subversion'. Article 79 of the 1967 constitution provides for the declaration of a state of siege, but as an extraordinary measure only 'in cases of international war or conflict, foreign invasion, internal turmoil or a grave threat from one of these'. The permanent use of the state of siege is clearly unconstitutional; Stroessner himself has repeatedly boasted that Paraguay has preserved internal peace better than any other country in South America. Its true function is to clamp down on all opposition to Stroessner's rule.

According to the interpretation of the Supreme Court, all individual rights may be suppressed if a state of siege is declared. Consequently, it has repeatedly rejected writs of habeas corpus brought to its attention on behalf of political detainees. As a result political prisoners have remained in jail for periods of up to twenty years without trial, detained 'at the President's request'.

## The Security Apparatus

The Ministry of the Interior, headed by Dr Sabino Augusto Montanaro, has traditionally provided the umbrella for the security apparatus. With a national network of undercover agents and paid informers, who do not appear on its payroll, the ministry carries out a highly efficient counter-intelligence operation against the political opposition. The police Investigations Department (DIPC), headed by Pastor Coronel, is the major operational unit for political repression. Its interrogation centre is staffed by some 50 experienced torturers. The Vigilance and Crime Division (D-3) of the DIPC, headed by Dr Victorino Oviedo Olmedo, houses the major torture centre in Paraguay.

Counter-intelligence against the Communist Party and other Marxist organizations is coordinated by the semi-autonomous Technical Division for the Repression of Communism, commonly referred to as the 'Technical Division' (DT) and headed by the shadowy Dr Antonio Campos Alum. The DT liaises both with the political section (D-3) of the DIPC and the military intelligence division (G-2) of the armed forces, headed by General Benito Guanes Serrano. At the same time, the DT provides the major institutional link between the Asunción CIA station and the Paraguayan security apparatus. Almost all the staff of the DT are US-trained.

Until the death of its head, General Patricio Colman, in 1972, the Fourteenth Infantry Regiment was the main operational unit for repression of independent peasant organizations. Since then, this role has been divided between a special unit within the Security Guard of the Police Force (GS) headed by Colonel Felix Grau and the Second Cavalry Division, based in Villarrica, headed by General Bernardino Valois Arza.

Local Colorado Party militias, known as the *Py-Nandu* (silent feet) provide a back-up security force at times of internal crisis. They determined the outcome of the 1947 civil war and subsequently wrought vengeance on the defeated opposition at a village level. They were again called into play during the search-

and-destroy operations against guerillas in 1959-60. After a long period of inactivity they were mobilized in Caaguazú in March 1980 for the repression of peasant organizations protesting against Brazilian landbuying in the region.

# Political Parties

### Colorado Party (Asociación Nacional Republicana — ANR)

One of the two traditional parties founded in 1870, it has been skillfully transformed into the official part of the dictatorship. It has a highly centralized and authoritarian structure, totally subservient to Stroessner. The party has an effective national organization through a network of *seccionales* (branches) which extend to village level in rural areas and neighbourhood level in towns. Party affiliation, which is computerized, is compulsory for all administrative and professional civil servants, including doctors and teachers. Party affiliation in rural areas is seen as an insurance policy to avoid constant harassment by local Colorado bosses, whose power often exceeds that of the mayor.

In recent years Colorado Party members have increasingly expressed discontent at abuses by local bosses and opportunists who joined the party since Stroessner came to power.

### Febrerista Party (Partido Revolucionario Febrerista — PRF)

This party originated in the revolt by demobilized soldiers after the Chaco War in 1936. It is a social democrat party, affiliated to the Socialist International. Although legally recognized, it is constantly under attack by the government. Its members were advised to cast blank votes in the 1978 presidential election. Its weekly paper, *El Pueblo*, is the only legal opposition newspaper in circulation.

The following parties are not recognized by the electoral board:

### Authentic Liberal Radical Party (PLRA)

When the major opposition Liberal Party declared its intention of abstaining from the 1978 presidential election, official recognition was granted to a handful of Liberals who were willing to participate. Official recognition was denied to the bulk of the party which then formed the PLRA and which advocates a more principled opposition to the dictatorship.

13

### Christian Democrat Party (PDC)

This party was founded in 1960 and is still denied electoral recognition although it is allowed to hold meetings.

The following parties are illegal:

### The Communist Party (PCP)

Founded in 1928, the PCP has only been legal for a nine-month period (1946-47). It has maintained an active presence within the country ever since Stroessner came to power, despite persistent repression. In 1978, three party leaders, Antonio Maidana, Alfredo Acorta and Julio Rojas, were released after 20 years imprisonment. In November 1975, the general secretary of the PCP, Dr Miguel Angel Soler, and two members of the central committee were brutally tortured to death following their discovery inside the country (see Appendix 2). The PCP is closely aligned with the Soviet Union and advocates a united front strategy for overthrowing Stroessner.

### Popular Colorado Movement (MOPOCP)

The MOPOCO was founded by Colorado dissidents in exile following Stroessner's take-over of the party in 1959. It maintains an active presence inside Paraguay. In 1973, MOPOCO split between a majority in favour of coordinated action with other opposition parties while a minority, later renamed 'ANR in exile', decided to work for an internal solution within the Colorado Party.

### The First of March Organization (OPM)

An embryonic armed opposition to the dictatorship emerged in the early 1970s, drawing its membership from peasant activists within the *ligas agrarias* and students influenced by events in neighbouring Argentina. The OPM suffered a severe setback in April 1976 when two of its leaders, Juan Carlos da Costa and Mario Schaerer, were wounded in a police siege and subsequently died under torture. In the ensuing repression, many OPM activists were arrested, sought political asylum or fled into clandestinity in Argentina.

# Trade Unions

## Paraguayan Confederation of Workers (CPT)

Following the defeat of the general strike in 1958 and the subsequent replacement of its leadership by government-appointed
nominees, the main trade union body, the CPT, was brought firmly
under the control of the Ministry of Justice and Labour. The
CPT receives a declared annual grant of US$8,000 from the
ministry, under whose name it is listed in the Asunción telephone
directory. Every year the CPT hierarchy declares Stroessner
'the nation's number one worker'.

Nevertheless, in recent years the rapid growth of trade union
membership as a result of the foreign investment boom, together
with the unaccustomed increase in the rate of inflation, have
created internal pressure for reform of the CPT. The CPT has also
come under international criticism. In November 1979 it was
expelled from the International Confederation of Free Trade
Unions, and hence from its Latin American regional affiliate
ORIT, on the grounds of political subservience. Shortly afterwards an internal power struggle led to a change in the leadership of the CPT. The new general secretary, Dr Modesto Ali,
promised a more independent position with regard to the government, but he has failed to carry this out.

In 1979 a reform movement, known as the 'Group of Nine',
emerged openly within the CPT. It includes the rapidly growing
construction workers and metal workers unions, as well as the
bank workers, print workers and journalists unions, and publishes
its own monthly broadsheet, *Trabajo*. As a result of pressure from
the Group of Nine, in February 1980 the council of delegates of
the CPT was convened for the first time since the 1958 general
strike. Delegates from 85 trade unions called on the CPT leadership to press for wage increases to compensate for the drop in real
wages in the previous two years and pressed for greater independence from government interference in union matters.

## National Coordination of Workers (CNT)

In 1963 the fledging Christian Democrat Party founded the
Christian Confederation of Workers (CCT) which concentrated its
activities on the organization of the church-sponsored peasant
leagues *(ligas agrarias)*. The CCT operated in a semi-clandestine

fashion and suffered heavily from periodic waves of repression. In December 1977, 19 trade union and peasant leaders linked to the CCT were arrested during a secret meeting held outside Asunción and several were badly tortured, including Victoriano Centurión, one of the founders of the *ligas agrarias*. They were released after an unprecedented display of international solidarity, which even included a visit from United States AFL-CIO trade union leaders. In 1978 the CCT merged with the small National Centre of Urban Workers (CNTU) to form the CNT and is now affiliated to the Christian Democrat regional trade union confederation for Latin America, CLAT.

# POWER GAME

## 'Discovery'

The original inhabitants of Paraguay were a semi-nomadic people, predominantly the Guaraní. The Spanish came to Paraguay in a fruitless search for gold. When their settlement at Buenos Aires was attacked by Indians they sought refuge in Asunción, which was founded in 1537. For the next fifty years Asunción was the headquarters of the Spanish conquest of the southern half of South America and a strategic outpost for repulsing Portuguese expansion westwards from Brazil.

Subsequently Paraguay became an economic backwater and remained very weakly integrated with the world economy throughout the colonial period. There were no mines nor plantations and consequently little immigration from Spain after the initial conquest. With no outlet to the sea, exports and imports were highly vulnerable to arbitrary river taxes imposed by Buenos Aires.

In the early seventeenth century, foreign Jesuits began to evangelize the Guaranís of eastern Paraguay who had fled from the area around Asunción after the Spanish conquest. They established autocratic but self-sufficient economic units in 30 fortified settlements with a combined population of 200,000.

Political tension arose between the Spanish and the Jesuits over the appropriation of Guaraní labour for the exploitation of *yerba maté* (a kind of tea), which was the main export during the colonial period. This erupted in the Comuneros Rebellion (1721-35) and was followed by a second Guaraní uprising against the proposed cession of seven Jesuit settlements to Portugal.

In the half century before independence the Paraguayan economy stagnated. Following the expulsion of the Jesuits in 1768 their settlements collapsed. In 1776 nominal control over Paraguay passed from Lima to the newly created Viceroyalty of Rio de la Plata, thus deepening its dependence on Buenos Aires.

After three centuries of external dependence, geographical isolation and a tradition of military preparedness, nationalist sentiment was running high in Paraguay as the Spanish Empire began to collapse at the beginning of the nineteenth century.

## Nationalist Development

*'I found he was not quite so deeply impressed as I would have wished with the importance of British commerce and British influence.'*
**R.B. Hughes, first British government representative in Paraguay, on meeting President Carlos Antonio López, October 1841.**

In May 1810 Argentina declared its independence from Spain and in July the Asunción city council rejected an Argentinian proposal for integration into an enlarged Argentine nation. In December a regiment was sent from Buenos Aires, supposedly to liberate Paraguay from the Spanish yoke. It received a hostile reception as soon as it crossed into Paraguayan territory and was forced to retreat ignominiously after two decisive defeats by a Paraguayan militia of 5,000 men. In both battles local *mestizo* officers and not Spanish troops provided the effective military leadership of the Paraguayan forces. In the struggle against Buenos Aires Paraguay was thus simultaneously ensuring its independence from Spain.

Paraguayan nationalists were finally provoked into action when the governor of Paraguay attempted to strengthen the position of the royalists by requesting military assistance from Portuguese troops in Brazil, ostensibly because of the continued military threat from Buenos Aires. On 14 May 1811 the Asunción barracks revolted and the governor was forced to capitulate. A series of congresses and juntas followed whose changing composition reflected the growing political ascendency of the nationalists over those who favoured a union with Buenos Aires. On 12 October 1812 a general congress finally proclaimed the Republic of Paraguay, the first in Latin America. Paraguay had now declared a triple independence: from Spain, Buenos Aires and Portugal.

Dr José Gaspar Rodrigues de Francia soon came to personify Paraguayan independence. For nearly 30 years his absolute and austere rule was responsible for welding the Paraguayan nation into being and providing a firm economic base for future development. Argentina still refused to recognize Paraguayan independence and hoped to incorporate her into an enlarged Argentinian nation. Buenos Aires pursued an economic blockade of Paraguayan trade and Paraguayan exports were either taxed out of existence or, as in the case of tobacco, were banned altogether. During this period Paraguay was also engaged in clashes with Portuguese troops on her northern border.

In the face of these threats to Paraguayan independence, Francia pursued a domestic policy of economic self-sufficiency and state control of the economy, together with the ruthless suppression of political opponents suspected of spying for Buenos Aires. He allied himself with the interests of the artisans and peasants, amongst whom support for the independence movement was strongest, and directed his repression against the urban bourgoisie in Asunción, mainly foreign traders of European origin who relied on credit from Buenos Aires for the financing of their operations. In 1814 all foreigners were made to declare their wealth and were subsequently bankrupted by a policy of taxation and forced loans to the state. They were also banned from posts in the state administration. The drastic reduction in foreign trade and lack of domestic investment opportunities also served to impoverish the bourgeoisie.

In pursuit of his policy of strengthening the economic interests of the peasants, in 1825 Francia ordered all private landowners to present titles to their land to prove their ownership. Many were unable to prove titles and their land passed to the state. In 1824 all church property, including their vast landholdings, was brought under state control. The state also possessed land formerly belonging to the Spanish crown or the Jesuits, as well as land confiscated from foreigners and Francia's political opponents, and it inherited property belonging to foreigners who died without Paraguayan-born heirs. Consequently by 1840 the state owned the whole of the Chaco as well as nearly half of the eastern region, including almost all the *yerba* plantations.

State control over agricultural production was extensive, with the objective of attaining self-sufficiency in food. By 1818 there were 50 large and 22 small state farms established on land suitable for livestock rearing. These well-organized farms eventually ended Paraguay's dependence on imported livestock; they were also used for feeding and equipping the army. Much state-owned land was rented for an unlimited period to peasant squatters who had traditionally occupied it.

The double legacy of the Francia period — widespread state control over the economic resources of the country and the increased social and ethnic homogeneity of the population — provided a firm foundation for the ambitious development strategy pursued by his successor, Carlos Antonio López.

The period 1842 to 1862 was undoubtedly the 'golden era' in Paraguayan history. In 1865, on the eve of the War of the Triple Alliance, Paraguay was generally recognized to be one of the most developed countries in South America and a major economic power within the sub-continent.

This rapid economic and social progress was to a great extent the product of the development philosophy of President López, who pursued a strategy of self-reliant economic development through extensive state intervention. Foreign technical expertise under state control was welcomed but there was no recourse to foreign private investment. This economic doctrine contrasted sharply with the laissez-faire liberalism prevalent among the ruling classes of the rest of South America, and the foreign press of the time created a very distorted and unfavourable image of Paraguay as a result.

In 1845 the first newspaper in Paraguay was founded and the first school books were printed. Free and obligatory primary education was introduced and technical schools set up. In 1855 the first teacher training college in Latin America was opened in Asunción. By 1862, the year López died, there were 435 schools and 24,500 pupils in Paraguay.

In 1846 all *yerba maté* and timber resources became the property of the state; by 1854 nearly 59% of all exports were accounted for by the state. Exploitation of the *yerbales* (plantations) was carried out by private citizens hiring a concession from the state. The state owned an estimated 1,000,000 head of cattle and exercised complete control over the sale of the major export commodities: *maté* and wood to Argentina, and cotton, tobacco and fruit to Europe. The state farms, another legacy of the Francia era, were extended to cover over 75% of the eastern region of the country. The value of foreign trade trebled between 1853 and 1859, and by 1860 Paraguay was running a large balance of trade surplus and was recognized in Europe as one of the leading trading nations of South America. Externally traded goods were shipped by the state-owned fleet of eleven steamships and 50 sailing vessels.

The construction of the first railway in the La Plata region (one of the first in South America) and the establishment of an iron foundry were the most famous material achievements of the López era. The first telegraph line in the La Plata region was also set up in Paraguay in 1864.

Public savings from state enterprises and the foreign exchange earnings of state-controlled foreign trade were the only sources of finance for this ambitious development programme. No recourse was made to foreign borrowing and private foreign investment was prohibited.

## The War of the Triple Alliance

'. . . a stubbornness of purpose, a savage valour and an enduring desperation rare in the annals of mankind.'
**Sir Richard Burton describing the struggle of Paraguay against the forces of the Triple Alliance in** Letters from the Battlefields of Paraguay, **London 1870.**

The War of the Triple Alliance was a turning-point in the history of Paraguay. The self-reliant development strategy of the previous fifty years was overthrown as a result of the war and replaced by a process of extreme economic dependence on the metropolitan countries.

Paraguay's foreign policy strategy ever since independence had been to maintain a balance of power between Argentina and Brazil in the La Plata region, as a means of safeguarding her own existence as an independent nation. Carlos Antonio López regarded the independence of Uruguay as fundamental in ensuring the equilibrium of political forces in the region. Any outside intervention in Uruguayan affairs was thus interpreted as an indirect attack on the sovereignty of Paraguay itself.

The interests of both Rio de Janeiro and Buenos Aires concided in their common desire to put a stop to the growing economic ascendency of Paraguay in the La Plata region. The evident success of Paraguay's self-reliant development had begun to jeopardize the hegemony which the privileged satellites of Rio de Janeiro and Buenos Aires exercised over their own hinterlands. Paraguay in its present form had to be erased as a potential ally for popular revolts in the Mato Grosso of Brazil or the Argentinian provinces.

War between Paraguay and Brazil broke out as a result of Brazilian military intervention in Uruguay in 1864 to overthrow the government of the ruling Blanco Party. The defeated Blancos requested Paraguayan assistance and when Argentina refused permission for Paraguayan troops to cross her territory en route for Uruguay, President Francisco Solano López of Paraguay declared war on Argentina as well.

In May 1865 Brazil, Argentina and the new Colorado government in Uruguay signed a secret pact, later known as the Treaty of the Triple Alliance, to overthrow the 'barbaric dictatorship' of Francisco Solano López and ostensibly to replace it with a democratic form of government. The real aims of the alliance were to wrest control of the basic economic resources of Paraguay from the state and to transfer them to Argentinian and European capitalists, and to annex large areas of Paraguayan territory, such as Misiones and parts of the Mato Grosso and the Chaco, which had long been coveted by Argentina and Brazil for strategic reasons. In both of its aims the alliance proved to be highly successful.

Britain, the most powerful imperial power in the region at the time, provided strong backing for the Triple Alliance. The allied war effort was largely financed by British banks. The existence of the 'secret' treaty itself was first made public in the British Parliament. Powerful British interests in Argentina and in the coffee-growing Mato Grosso stood to gain from an allied victory which would open up Paraguay's rivers to international traffic. The British diplomatic representative in Buenos Aires, Edward Thornton, who regularly attended meetings of the Argentinian cabinet, was outspoken in his contempt for Solano López and in his support for the allied cause.

After five years of bitter struggle, in which women and children fought alongside the Paraguayan troops, defeat finally came on 1 March 1870 when López himself was killed in battle at Cerro Corá in the far north of Paraguay. The population of around 500,000 in 1865, had been reduced five years later to 250,000, of whom only 28,000 were adult males. The economy was prostrate; the railway and iron foundry had been completely destroyed by Brazilian troops. Asunción was sacked and plunder removed by ship to Buenos Aires. Some 55,000 square miles, equivalent to over a quarter of its pre-war territory, had been lost for ever; 60% went to Argentina and 40% to Brazil.

# 'From Independence to Dependence'

*'The number of Englishmen in Paraguay is still small but the British capital already invested in that country is very considerable and far exceeds in amount the investments of all other European nations combined. The steamers navigating the great rivers are British; the railway is British and so are the tramways. Most of the banking capacity of the country is British and a considerable proportion of the public lands has become the property of British bondholders.'*

From *Paraguay – The Land and the People, Natural Wealth and Commerical Capabilities*, by **Dr E. de Bourgade la Dardye, London 1892.**

Defeat in the War of the Triple Alliance heralded the denationalization of the Paraguayan economy. The autonomous development process was erased and replaced by a dependent growth pattern and increasing foreign control of the nation's economic resources.

Following the departure of the Brazilian occupying forces in 1876, a new dependent *caudillo* elite, composed mostly of Paraguayan traitors who had fought alongside the forces of the Triple Alliance against López, grouped themselves into two opposing clubs which in 1887 were formally declared political parties: the Liberals and the Colorados (respectively the blues and the reds). The two factions were not divided by ideological differences, since both were essentially lasissez-faire parties promoting the economic interests of the elite, which itself acted on behalf of foreign capitalists.

The two parties reflected the international rivalry for political control over Paraguay, with Anglo-Argentinian capital generally supporting the Liberals and Brazilian interests supporting the Colorados. The Colorados were in power until 1904; thereafter the Liberals ruled until 1940. However, the period from 1870 to 1940 was marked by a tumultuous series of coups, counter-coups, palace 'revolutions', and two-day presidents as rival groups within the elite fought over the rich pickings to be gained from foreign economic domination.

In 1871 and 1872 the puppet government set up in Asunción by the victorious allies agreed to the floating of two issues of public bonds for 'national reconstruction' on the London markets, with par values of £1 million and £500,000. To secure these loans the Paraguayan government pledged its customs, general revenues, public lands, railways and all public buildings as collateral. In fact only £400,000 and £125,000 respectively actually reached Paraguay and most of this disappeared into politicians' pockets. The Paraguayan nation was saddled with a huge foreign debt, and from 1874 onwards was in default on repayment of the loans. In 1889 the state-owned railway, symbol of Paraguay's economic independence, was handed over to British capitalists on give-away terms, as compensation to the 1871-72 bondholders.

In 1883 and 1885 laws were passed permitting the sale of state-owned land to foreign capitalists at extremely low prices. In the next 15 years the majority of Paraguay's state-owned lands were sold off to foreign capitalists, mainly Argentinian and British. In 1885 and 1886 alone over 114,700 square kilometres of Chaco land, comprising 35% of the area of the country, were sold off to a mere 60 individuals or companies. These huge land sales provided the basis for the system of highly unequal distribution of land and irrational exploitation of the country's natural resources, which became a characteristic feature of Paraguayan agriculture.

As late as 1946, only 25, almost exclusively foreign companies still owned a third of the total land area of Paraguay; two of these, the British-owned *Industrial Paraguaya* and *Carlos Casado*, together owned 13% of the area.

## The Chaco War

The ruling Liberal Party was already riddled with internal divisions when in December 1928 skirmishes broke out between Paraguayan and Bolivian forces in the Chaco. Despite the steady advance of Bolivian troops towards Asunción during 1929 and 1930 the government pursued a policy of appeasement and information concerning the extent of the Bolivian penetration was concealed from the general public. When war finally broke out in July 1932, Bolivian troops were only 130 miles from Asunción.

The Chaco War (1932-35), coming at a time of increasing world protectionism, brought to a head growing discontent in Paraguay against the lasissez-faire liberalism of the past 60 years and provoked the first rupture with the traditional two party system. Intellectual groups which had emerged in Asunción in the late 1920s gave birth to a new populist political party later to be known as the Febrerista Party. During the war itself, however, a deceptive sense of national unity kept the discontent simmering below the surface.

The conventional explanation of the cause of the Chaco War is the Bolivian desire to obtain a secure trade route to the Atlantic following the loss of her outlet to the Pacific as a result of her defeat by Chile in the War of the Pacific (1879-83). However, this explanation ignores the extremely high transport costs of exporting minerals across the enormous distance between the Bolivian altiplano and the Atlantic coast and the fact that the River Pilcomayo, which flows from Bolivia across the Chaco and into the River Paraguay, is either dry or unnavegable for most of the year. Economic conflict over the oil resources of the Chaco and the interests of foreign capital in the region provide a more convincing explanation.

During the 1920s foreign capitalists consolidated their control over the Chaco lands so that by 1928, when the first clashes broke out between Paraguay and Bolivia, the capital investment of the foreign companies in the region exceeded US$10 million, with at least one half of the total area of the Chaco's 23.5 million hectares directly controlled by Argentinian companies.

By 1926 Standard Oil had a virtual monopoly of oil concessions in Bolivia. They had bought up a total of 7 million hectares in south-east Bolivia, including one concession of 2 million hectares purchased for US$2 million from Spruille Braden, who later became United States ambassador to the Chaco Peace Conference. Standard Oil built two small refineries to commercialize the oil discovered in their concession area, but the expansion of petroleum production for export was restricted by the lack of an available route to the Atlantic seaboard. The war was most probably precipitated by Bolivia's desire, encouraged by Standard Oil, to obtain an outlet to the La Plata region and the Atlantic seaboard specifically for petroleum exports rather than for exports in general, and at the same time to ensure sovereignty over possible oil deposits further south in the Chaco.

In 1934 Standard Oil was accused by Senator Huey Long of Louisiana in the United States Senate of having aided the Bolivian war effort in order to obtain access to a port on the River Paraguay by influencing the flotation of huge Bolivian bond issues on the New York stock market in pre-Depression days. By 1926 some 65% of all Bolivian government revenues were committed to servicing foreign loans for which she had pledged her national bank, custom and tax receipts as collateral. Yet Bolivia was nevertheless able to raise two more loans of US$13.6 million in 1927 and US$22.8 million in 1928 from Dillon Read and Co. of New York. In 1932 another US$20 million was advanced by a consortium of New York bankers for the purchase of arms in the USA despite the fact that, in strictly commerical terms, Bolivia was a very poor risk as she had already declared a moratorium on foreign debt repayments.

Paraguayan knowledge of the Chaco terrain and the guerilla warfare tactics used by her troops, overcame Bolivia's numerically superior armed forces and greater fire-power. At the end of three years of heavy fighting the Paraguayan army was able to repel the Bolivian forces from almost the whole of the Chaco region, back to the foothills  of the Andes. The war cost the lives of 45,000 Paraguayans and 55,000 Bolivians.

As the military victory of Paraguay became assured, the growing divisions in Paraguayan society rose to the surface. Memories of the ineptitude of the Liberals' preparation for war, and the knowledge that leading Liberal politicians were making fortunes out of the war through their links with foreign companies under contract to supply arms and provisions, increased resentment against the Liberal government.

The final straw was the armistice which the Liberal government signed on 12 June 1935, ostensibly because their lines were overextended, just when it seemed that the Bolivians were about to surrender.

The military coup of 17 February 1936 (from which the Febrerista Party gets its name) by anti-Liberal army officers initially met with support from 100,000 war veterans who were still armed, and from other opposition groups. These soon achieved majority representation in the cabinet of Colonel Rafael Franco, the popular hero of the Chaco War who became president. One of the first acts of the new government was to rehabilitate the memory of ex-president Francisco Solano López, who had been the object of derision throughout the Liberal era. The most important measure of the Febrerista government during its brief existence was the land reform law. About 180,000 hectares were expropriated in only fifteen months and titles granted to some 10,000 families. However, in the face of strong pressure from the organized working class, the Febrerista government jailed labour leaders and closed down left-wing newspapers.

By the time the armistice had been signed in June 1935, the Paraguayan front line had advanced to within sight of the oil rigs of Standard Oil in the extreme north-west Chaco. Standard Oil therefore began to press for Argentinian support in forcing Paraguay to accept a final border line sufficiently to the south-east so that her own oil interests would not be threatened by Paraguayan troops. Spruille Braden was appointed as US ambassador to the Chaco Peace Conference set up in Buenos Aires to work out a final agreement.

Braden stated that the Peace Conference should if necessary make a declaration placing the blame on Paraguay for failing to come to an agreement. More specifically he suggested that 'the threat of a Conference declaration along the above lines might bring Paraguay to heel. It is even possible that its issuance would upset the Franco regime bringing in other politicians who would be willing to compromise and effect a settlement.' This wish later came true when there was a volte-face in Paraguay's hard-line attitude to the terms of a peace treaty following the defeat of the Franco regime and the return to power of the Liberal Party. On 12 August 1937 the Liberal commander of the armed forces in the Chaco, Colonel Ramón Paredes, led a successful coup against the Febrerista government thus re-installing the Liberal regime. The final peace treaty, signed on 21 July 1938, showed that it was precisely in the west of the Chaco where the oil deposits lay that Paraguay yielded territory behind her cease-fire lines. Whilst Paraguay secured the great bulk of the Chaco, the very land which Paraguay had annexed during the war and which was ceded to Bolivia on signing the treaty was that land west of Villazón which later became the booming centre of the Bolivian petroleum industry.

## The Rise of Stroessner

The return to power of the Liberals was short-lived. Following the sudden death of Chaco War leader President Estigarribia, his former Minister of War, General Higinio Morinigo, assumed power in 1940. He banned all political parties and severely repressed the trade union movement. The Allied victory provoked a military movement in 1946 against the fascist backers of Morinigo, who was forced to accept a Colorado-Febrerista coalition government under his nominal control. This brief period of political freedom saw intense political activity as the previously banned parties vied with each other other to fill the political vacuum. Endangered by the rising tide of popular mobilization and growth of left-wing parties, Morinigo excluded the Febrerista Party from the government and openly sided with the Colorados. This instantly polarized political opinion and a civil war broke out in March 1947 in which the Colorados triumphed over the combined forces of Liberals, Febreristas and Communists. In the ensuing havoc, armed Colorado militias wrought vengeance on their defeated opponents throughout the country, producing the first wave of mass emigration to Argentina.

A series of coups and counter-coups followed as rival factions in the Colorado Party, the *democráticos* (moderates) and *guionistas* (extremists), vied for political power. Meanwhile a young army officer, Alfredo Stroessner, was consolidating his own military power base, gaining promotion by adroitly switching allegiance between the factions.

Stroessner was born of a German father and Paraguayan mother in Encarnación in 1912. He joined the army at the age of 16, becoming a cadet at the military school in Asunción. He fought in the Chaco War, becoming a military officer in 1932. In 1940 he went on an artillery course in Brazil and in 1944 became commander of the First ('General Bruguez') Regiment of Artillery, enabling him to play an important role in the 1947 civil war as a supporter of Morinigo. He rose rapidly under the *democrático* government of President Chávez (1950-54) and was appointed commander-in-chief of the armed forces in October 1951 at the age of 38. From this position he began encouraging splits within the Chávez government by fomenting criticism of its mild attempts at economic planning and greater trade links with Peronist Argentina. In June 1953 Stroessner visited the United States for the first time, as the guest of army secretary Robert Stephens. Less than a year later, on 4 May 1954, he deposed Chávez in a military coup.

## Consolidation of Power

By identifying himself with the Colorado Party Stroessner secured a popular base for his regime, a key difference from other military dictatorships in Latin America, and one which has contributed to

28

his political longevity. A party convention nominated him as Colorado presidential candidate and the elections were held in July 1954 with Stroessner as the sole candidate. In 1956 Stroessner forced into exile his arch rival within the Colorado Party, Epifanio Méndez Fleitas, a populist leader who advocated structural reform and economic planning in favour of the poor. Stroessner was now free to impose an IMF-inspired stabilization plan which involved a wage freeze and reduction in public subsidies. This led to a drop in real incomes and growing labour unrest in Asunción. A general strike was crushed in August 1958 when police arrested 300 trade union leaders and placed police officers in key trade union posts; in response the Congress called for political normalization. In April 1959 the state of siege, which had been in force since Stroessner came to power, was lifted and a month of demonstrations and street battles between police and students followed. When the lower house voted by a narrow majority in May to condemn police brutality Stroessner dissolved Congress, re-imposed the state of siege and sent the army to occupy Asunción. 400 Colorado politicians opposed to Stroessner were imprisoned or fled into exile, where they formed MOPOCO (Popular Colorado Movement) under the leadership of Méndez Fleitas.

Stroessner now set about converting the purged Colorado Party into a fascist-style party swearing blind allegiance to himself. The party structure was re-organized along authoritarian and verticalist lines. Party affiliation was later computerized and the membership organized through a national network of *seccionales* (branches) which extended to village level in rural areas and neighbourhood level in urban areas and part of whose work was the regular surveillance of opposition activity.

Affiliation to the Colorado Party was made obligatory for all public employees, teachers and officials in the armed forces, as well as for doctors, engineers, economists and architects employed in the public sector. Purchase of the Colorado Party daily paper, *Patria*, became compulsory for all civil servants, with payment deducted automatically from wage packets. A personality cult was built up around the figure of Stroessner in an attempt to identify him with the nationalist heroes of Paraguayan history. Photographs and busts of Stroessner are now displayed in all public offices as well as in most private companies. In all major professional and student bodies, Stroessner-backed parallel associations were set up in order to wrest control from potential opponents.

## The Stagnant Years

Despite the offical rhetoric of 'peace and progress', the economic growth rate from 1954 until 1973 hardly matched the increase in population and real incomes stagnated as a result. The structure of production remained unchanged as a consequence of the grossly unequal system of land tenure and the rapid growth of smuggling. Economic power under Stroessner became consolidated in an alliance between *latifundistas* (large landowners) and neo-Colorados, a civil and military clique who invested their new fortunes, derived from administrative corruption and smuggling, in buying rural properties for cattle ranching, thereby reinforcing the inequality of land tenure.

The regime's model of 'outward oriented growth' became the economic expression of this alliance. It advocated export-led growth, an open-door policy to foreign investment and rejected any move in favour of import substitution since this would involve curbs on smuggling. The share of the industrial sector in total national output remained constant at around only 13% since domestic manufacturers were unable to compete with smuggled imports of basic goods from Argentina and Brazil, and consumer goods from all over the world. The fledgling national business class remained on the political sidelines.

Foreign aid inflows have been an important source of support for the ruling elite through road building and assistance to cattle ranchers, but despite generous tax concessions, few foreign companies were attracted to Paraguay at this time due to its isolation, poor communications and tiny domestic market. Most of the foreign investment went into agriculture; English, Argentine and American companies bought up huge tracts of land for cattle ranching, *yerba maté*, timber and tannin extraction. The British company, Brooke Bond Liebig, also set up a large meat-packing factory in Asunción (see box).

However, as we shall see, in the mid-1970s the pattern of foreign investment changed and increased enormously at the same time; companies moved out of traditional areas of investment into

30

# FINE CATTLE
# ...IN PARAGUAY

# GOOD FOOD
# ...IN BRITAIN

Because the grasslands of Paraguay can nourish millions of cattle, a massive
meat-packing factory has been built up by Liebig's Extract of Meat Company,
whose products add both nourishment and richer flavours to the world's cooking.
Liebig's, a subsidiary of the Brooke Bond Liebig Group, looks forward to
handling an increasing supply of fine Paraguayian cattle, so helping to maintain
and improve the economy of the lovely country immortalised by
its President, Don Alfredo Stroessner, in one simple but
memorable phrase, "The People and the land are Paraguay"

*"The People and the land are Paraguay"*

## Liebig's in Paraguay
PARTNERS IN A NATION'S PROGRESS

Brooke Bond Liebig closed the factory mentioned in this advertisement
in 1978, but they continue to have considerable economic interests in
Paraguay.

agribusiness projects in the eastern border region and other transnational companies moved into Paraguay for the first time.

Primary product exports (tobacco, corned beef, *yerba maté* and tannin) stagnated in these years and the index of per capita food production fell from 100 in 1957-59 to only 83 in 1969. This is despite the fact that Paraguay has one of the highest ratios of cultivable land per capita in the world. Only 2.2% of the total land area was under cultivation in 1970 while it is estimated that nine times this area is suitable for arable farming. Yet despite this superabundance of available land 70% of the population have to scratch a living on tiny eroded *minifundio* plots, while in 1956 106 owners accounted for 40% of all land in Paraguay excluding the Chaco.

This unequal system of land tenure has resulted in a massive emigration of the rural poor and landless to neighbouring countries. By the early 1970s there were an estimated 800,000 Paraguayans in Argentina alone and another 200,000 in Brazil and Uruguay. Cheap Paraguayan labour has traditionally been the mainstay of the construction industry in Buenos Aires and provides a large share of the domestic servants. A common Paraguayan saying is, 'the slums of Paraguay are to be found in Argentina'. In 1979 one quarter of all Paraguayans were living outside the country, representing the highest rate of emigration in Latin America.

## Opposition

The poor peasantry, supported by the church, provided the only serious opposition to the regime during this period. A grass-roots social movement emerged in the early 1960s known as the *ligas agrarias* (agrarian leagues). They represented a reaction by land-hungry *campesinos* (peasants) to the grossly unequal system of land tenure. The *ligas* were non-violent and Christian-based and received considerable support from the Catholic church during the 1960s. By 1969 they had an estimated membership of over 20,000, organized in a series of communities throughout the countryside and operating small producer and distribution co-operatives. As the movement began to sap the Colorado Party of its traditional support among the peasant masses, the authorities began to harass the *ligas* under the pretext that they were communist-inspired. There was a wave of repression of the *ligas* throughout the country in 1975-76. Some 50 peasant leaders were killed, hundreds fled into exile and over 5,000 were arrested. *Liga* communities were split up and families transported to distant parts of the country in order to destroy the movement. As a result the *liga* movement was forced into clandestiny. By 1980 it was active in defending poor peasants in eastern Paraguay from land evictions (see page 56).

The church itself has been much weakened by recurring repression and expulsions as a result of its support for the *ligas* and its stand on human rights. The Paraguayan church began to adopt increasingly progressive stands on social issues in the light of the conclusions of the conference of Latin American bishops at Medellín in 1968. In December 1968 the 44th Assembly of the Paraguayan Bishops Conference (CEP) agreed to make a public stand on the question of political prisoners, and through its weekly paper *Comunidad* intensify its campaign against corruption and injustice. In 1969 the church supported protest demonstrations against the visit of Nelson Rockefeller to Paraguay. In the same year, the Jesuit priest Francisco de Paulo Oliva supported student protests against attacks by plaincothes police on fellow students and members of the church. Subsequently he was deported and a demonstration by priests and nuns in response was violently suppressed. As a result various government authorities were excommunicated.

In 1976 church-state relations deteriorated further still when the police invaded the school of Cristo Rey and the residence of the Jesuits who ran the school and later expelled a large number of priests from the country. In response to this repression, representatives of the Catholic church, the German Evangelical church and the church of the Disciples of Christ (USA) decided in mid-1976 to form an inter-church committee to provide emergency help to political prisoners and their relatives. The Anglican church, with a history of over a century of missionary work in Paraguay, refused to participate in the committee and accused its members of being communists. It also claimed that to participate in the committee's work would prejudice its activities in the country, particularly the Anglican school, St Andrews, which is attended by the children of many government ministers including President Stroessner's grandson.

Although the church continues to be one of the main sources

of institutional opposition to the regime, repression has weakened it considerably and placed its future work in some doubt. In October 1978, peasants from the diocese of Coronel Oviedo sent a letter to the bishops meeting in Puebla, Mexico, in which they emphasized the plight of the repressed Paraguayan peasantry and their concern for the growing neglect of their rights by the church.

Opposition to the regime has also been found amongst certain sectors of the student movement. There are two universities in Paraguay, the National University of Asunción (founded in 1889) and the Catholic University (founded in 1962), with a total of about 10,000 students. The Catholic University, which is a private institution supported financially by international Catholic bodies, has managed to maintain some independence. The National University, however, is staffed mainly by members of the Colorado Party and since 1959 elections to the university union have been manipulated by massive enrolments of pseudo students paid by the Colorado Party, many of whom are members of the secret police. In response to government action, non-Colorado students formed the Independent Student Movement in 1965. This union has since been branded as 'subversive' and many of its leaders arrested. In July 1977 a number of its members and other intellectuals associated with a quarterly cultural magazine, *Criterio*, were arrested. They included Juan Felix Bogado, a university lecturer and co-founder of the Independent Student Movement; he was released after two years in prison. *Criterio* was subsequently closed down; it was the country's only serious magazine, critically examining the social and economic changes affecting Paraguay and drawing attention to the terms of the Itaipú treaty and the way the government was prejudicing the country's future economic development (see page 48).

Armed opposition has not posed a major challenge to the regime. The first attempt at armed struggle against Stroessner was a series of abortive guerilla invasions in December 1959 and April 1960. These were led by members of the Liberal Party who formed the 14 May Movement (*Movimento 14 de Mayo*) and members of the Communist Party calling themselves the United Front for National Liberation (*Frente Unido de Liberación Nacional* — FULNA). Both movements were brutally repressed. In the early 1970s some students attempted to construct a student-peasant alliance advocating armed resistance against the regime;

and in 1974 a group of students and some politicized members of the *ligas* formed an armed organization, the OPM (1March Organization). It grew very rapidly but was infiltrated by government agents from the beginning; in 1976 key leaders were killed in a wave of repression before it had a chance to put its aims into practice.

## Repression

The official justification for political repression in Paraguay is that that it is necessary in order to combat terrorism. However, Paraguay has remained virtually immune from the political turbulence of neighbouring countries over the past decade. No aircraft has ever been hijacked in Paraguay. The only assassination of a political figure was in June 1976 when a Croatian extremist harboured by the Stroessner regime gunned down the Uruguayan ambassador in an Asunción street after mistaking him for the Yugoslav ambassador. The only case of political kidnapping, that of a British executive of Brooke Bond Liebig in August 1973, was carried out by relatives of Interior Minister Sabino Montanaro, and officals of the Colorado Party itself.

The real purpose of repression is to forestall rather than to destroy political opposition. In this respect the Stroessner regime has been largely successful through its strategy of 'preventive repression', first publicly revealed at the 1972 Inter-American Defense Board meeting in Montevideo by General Johannsen and later adopted by several other countries in the Southern Cone. This strategy involves nipping in the bud any signs of growing militancy among independent groups outside direct government control by mass arrests aimed at frightening off potential dissidents. This strategy has been used constantly throughout Stroessner's 26-year rule.

Thanks to this strategy of preventive repression there exists in Paraguay today a culture of fear, a suspicion of outsiders and a degree of self-censorship in daily social intercourse incomparable with anywhere else in Latin America. Over 60% of the population were born after Stroessner took power and have known no other

*Continued on page 38.*

## Anti-Communists, Nazis and Somoza

The 12th congress of the World Anti-Communist League (WACL), whose headquarters are in South Korea, took place in Asunción in April 1979, attended by 400 delegates from 80 countries. Meeting in what they called 'this capital of freedom and anti-communism', the congress appealed to Latin American countries to update and strengthen the pacts for continental defence. Delegates agreed to put pressure on their respective governments to support the military regimes of Paraguay, Uruguay, Chile, Brazil, Argentina and Somoza's Nicaragua, which represent the 'regional vanguard' in the active fight against communism.

The congress elected as its new president Dr Juan Manuel Frutos, head of Paraguay's Rural Welfare Institute (IBR) since its foundation in 1963; he has made a fortune out of the sale of state lands to Brazilian land companies. Other members of the 16-man Paraguayan branch of the WACL include:

— General Benito Guanes Serrano, head of military intelligence (G-2).
— Pastor Coronel, head of the police Investigations Department (DIPC).
— Dr Antonio Campos Alum, head of the Technical Division for the Repression of Communism (DT).
— Anibal Fernández, Stroessner's press chief, responsible for newspaper censorship.
— Dr Manfredo Ramírez Russo, right-wing Catholic ideologue and land speculator, responsible for the repression of the progressive wing of the Catholic church.
— Nicanor Fleitas, until 1978 head of the tightly-controlled Paraguayan Confederation of Workers (CPT) and owner of a bus company.

Paraguay was an appropriate choice for a WACL congress. For several years the South American division of the WACL has operated a finance company in Asunción, *Financiera Urundey*, as a conduit for laundering funds from WACL's Saudi Arabian backers through Paraguay's free foreign exchange market for covert operations throughout the globe. Stroessner is a long-standing member of the WACL and under his regime the country has become a refuge and rendezvous for right-wing extremists from all over the world.

After the Second World War, many hundreds of Nazis from Europe sought refuge in Paraguay in isolated agricultural colonies. The most infamous is Dr Joseph Mengele, known as the 'Angel of Death' in Auschwitz concentration camp, who is featured in the best-selling novel and film *The Boys from Brazil*. Following the abduction of Adolf Eichmann in Argentina, Mengele left that country and crossed over to Paraguay in May 1959. He was granted Paraguayan citizenship by the Supreme Court in November; in his petition for citizenship he did not even bother to use an assumed name.

Since 1964 the governments of West Germany and Israel have repeatedly requested the extradition of Mengele but without success. In December 1977 Domingo Laino, in a motion to Congress, requested an enquiry into the granting of Paraguayan nationality to Mengele, but Stroessner's ruling Colorado Party blocked the motion. International pressure mounted in the weeks leading up to Stroessner's celebration of 25 years of dictatorial rule in August 1979. On 3 August 57 US congressmen sent him a telegram protesting his continued protection of Mengele and on 12 August the Paraguayan Supreme Court suddenly revoked Mengele's citizenship after finding him guilty of war crimes, something which had taken them seventeen years.

In August 1977 another wanted Nazi, former SS Captain Eduard Roschmann, the 'Butcher of Riga' whose atrocities are retold in Frederick Forsyth's *The Odessa File*, died in an Asunción hospital. In the few days before his identity was confirmed, Emilio Wolff, a former concentration camp inmate and member of Paraguay's tiny Jewish community, swore to the press that he would recognise Roschmann if he passed him in the street. The night his statements were published, Wolff's home was sprayed with bullets from a passing car.

More evidence of a continuing neo-Nazi presence in Paraguay is supplied by periodic announcements in the official press of visits to Stroessner by Colonel Hans Rudel, a Luftwaffe pilot and Hitler's most decorated officer and a well-known neo-Nazi in the West German army. On 21 April 1978 neo-Nazis in Paraguay organized a public meeting on the case of Rudolph Hess.

Two heads of the Italian fascist organization, *Ordine Nuovo*, Elio Massagrande and Gaetano Orlando, wanted in Italy for the July 1976 murder of a magistrate, have also been given protection in Paraguay, despite appeals by Interpol for their extradition. In September 1977 Stroessner invited Mirko Tremaglia, leader of the neo-fascist movement, *Movimento Sociale Italiano*, to lecture to the youth wing of the Colorado Party.

Another fascist organization which uses Paraguay as a safe base is the ultra right-wing Croatian autonomy movement. Croatian extremists first made contact with Stroessner's entourage during his private visit to Bavaria in July 1973. The Croatians were seeking refuge following their attack on the Yugoslav embassy in Stockholm. Ten were granted asylum in Paraguay and hired to train Stroessner's personal bodyguard, the *Batallón Escolta*. Their leader, Tony Zarisch, opened a karate school and was soon training torturers from the police Investigations Department in 'self-defence'.

Stroessner's latest 'guest' is Anastasio Somoza, the deposed dictator of Nicaragua, who arrived in Paraguay on 19 August 1979 in a chartered jet belonging to the Paraguayan state airline LAP and flown by Stroessner's personal pilot. With an entourage of 20 friends and relatives, Somoza made himself a home in a mansion which formerly served as the South African embassy. Stroessner granted Somoza political asylum and provided him with a group of army officers to act as aides-de-camp. Somoza has invested in real estate in Asunción and has bought a 8,000 hectare cattle ranch in the Chaco. Customers are still cleared out of supermarkets and restaurants every time Somoza decides to shop or dine.

system of government. Consequently, several 'typical' features of Latin American society have been completely absent in Paraguay since 1960. Street marches and open-air public meetings by opposition political parties, for instance, are unheard of. Political graffiti on walls are nowhere to be seen and anything remotely indentifiable as Marxist literature is absent from bookshops.

There has been no significant resistance to the Stroessner dictatorship since the guerilla invasions in 1959-60 were mercilessly crushed. Stroessner's orders at the time to take no prisoners alive have acted as a deterrent ever since.

## Political Imprisonment and Torture

The basic mechanisms for enforcing the strategy of preventive repression are the imprisonment and torture of Paraguayan citizens; they have been a notorious feature of Paraguayan life ever since Stroessner took power. Every year thousands of Paraguayans pass through the infamous police Investigations Department which is situated only two blocks away from the parliament building. There are periodic mass arrests when the Investigations Department fills to overflowing and temporary accommodation is sought elsewhere. The largest wave of arrests in recent years took place in April and May 1976 when over 2,000 peasants were detained and a temporary prison camp was opened at Emboscada.

The large majority of prisoners are detained for short periods only. Nevertheless, from 1960-77 there was a fluctuating long-term prison population of around 600, many of whom were detained for over ten years. Most of these long-term political prisoners were held in police stations in the suburbs of Asunción. Pressure from foreign governments has resulted in a sharp drop in the number of long-term political prisoners to around 30 in mid-1980. However, Paraguay still has the longest serving political prisoners in South America: Napoleon Ortigoza and Escolástico Ovando, both of whom have been detained since 1962.

The trial of political prisoners is a very recent phenomenon in Paraguay and is still confined to a tiny minority of those arrested. These have been tried under the draconian anti-subversive Law 209. Signed confessions extracted under torture provide the basis for the prosecution's case in all of these trials. Alfonso Silva and his wife Saturnina Almada were released in February 1978 after spending ten years in jail without trial. They were re-arrested in May 1979 and charged under Law 209 for acts allegedly committed in 1960, ten years before the law was passed.

The torture of political prisoners during the initial period of interrogation, or even before interrogation takes place, is common in Paraguay. It is used more as a deterrent and punishment and as a means of extracting signatures to false confessions than as a means of forcing detainees to disclose information. The most common methods of torture are the *pileta*, a bathtub containing water filled with filth and excrement in which the victim is submerged until he or she loses consciousness, and the application of electric shocks to sensitive parts of the body with a prod-like instrument called the *picana eléctrica*. It is impossible to determine the number of persons who have died under torture since Stroessner came to power as the lack of an independent judiciary and the fear of reprisals have left many cases undocumented. Amnesty International has published details of ten deaths under torture in 1976 alone. In October 1979 Amnesty International forwarded to the Paraguayan Supreme Court a vivid report on the death under torture of Dr Miguel Angel Soler, general secretary of the Paraguayan Communist Party, and two other members of its central committee, Derliz Villagra and Ruben González who had all disappeared in Asunción in November 1975. The Ministry of the Interior denied in a press statement that they had ever been arrested. In March 1980 *El Pueblo* published a letter from a fisherman in Argentina denouncing the discovery of their mutilated bodies floating in the River Paraguay in April 1976. (See Appendix 2).

In December 1978, 400 people attended a national human rights congress in Asunción organized by the Commission for the Defense of Human Rights in Paraguay, which was founded by Dr Carmen Casco de Lara Castro in June 1967. The findings of the congress noted that human rights continued to be grossly violated, torture of newly arrested detainees was still standard practice and there was considerable harassment of released prisoners.

## Disappearances

The disappearance of political opponents has occured throughout Stroessner's rule, although the numbers have increased considerably in recent years. Relatives of missing persons and the few lawyers who take up their cases meet a wall of silence. Writs of habeas corpus on their behalf go unanswered and inquiries at police stations generally yield no information. In 1978 Amnesty International published detailed cases of 20 persons who had disappeared over the previous three years. Four of these were already in police custody when they disappeared. In September 1976, over 300 political prisoners were transferred from the police Investigations Department to a prison camp at Emboscada. Four of these prisoners — Benjamin Ramírez Villalba, Rodolfo Ramírez Villalba, Amilcar Oviedo and Carlos Mancuello — never arrived at Emboscada and nothing has been heard of them since. The four had been detained since November 1974 and until the day before their disappearance Mancuello's mother regularly took him food and clothing.

There are very few cases of disappeared prisoners re-appearing. In May 1976 peasant leader Doroteo Brandel was arrested by army personnel after he had led a protest against the eviction of poor farmers in his village to make way for a Brazilian land company. His disappearance was reported in the press and denounced by the

Catholic church. After a writ of habeas corpus was submitted, the Supreme Court requested information about this prisoner from the armed forces. The answer to the court, signed by General Carpinelli, the commander of the Second Infantry Division, stated that Brandel was 'not known'. However, a British tourist, Alan Kent, who was arrested in Paraguay in December 1976 after complaining that a policeman had stolen his money, later testified to having shared a cell with Brandel in the headquarters of the Second Infantry Division, whose commander had denied any knowledge of him.

According to this testimony, Brandel had been alone for eight months in a tiny cell in very harsh conditions. Following international concern, Brandel was released in July 1978. One month later he returned to Asunción to denounce what happened to him (see Appendix 3) and to seek redress for his village. On 21 August 1978 he was shot in the back and stabbed seventeen times by assassins hired by General Carpinelli. The Paraguayan government attributed Brandel's death to a 'pub brawl'.

## Collaboration with Neighbouring Countries

Collaboration between the forces of repression in Paraguay and in neighbouring countries is very close indeed. Since 1973 there have been many reported cases of Argentinians disappearing in Paraguay and being handed over to the Argentine government. Similarly there has been an upsurge in the number of reported cases of Paraguayans disappearing in Argentina and being handled over to the Paraguayan authorities, after which they either disappear or appear later in Paraguayan jails. In February 1977 Dr Agustín Goiburú, an exiled doctor and leader of the MOFOCO dissident Colorado opposition to Stroessner, was kidnapped in Paraná by uniformed soldiers of the Argentinian army, who beat him up in the street and forced him into a vehicle. He was subsequently handed over to the Paraguayan authorities at a border crossing and taken to Asunción, since when he has disappeared. A month later Gustavo Edison Insaurralde, a leader of the Uruguayan national union of teachers was kidnapped in Asunción by Paraguayan police. According to enquiries made by the Catholic church,

*Continued on page 43.*

## Stroessner and South Africa

Since April 1974, when Stroessner, accompanied by a 100-strong Paraguayan delegation, became the first non-African head of state to visit South Africa in 20 years, economic and political relations between the two countries have expanded rapidly. After this visit the South African government agreed to finance the construction of Stroessner's new Palace of Justice and a 14-storey Foreign Ministry building with soft loans totalling US$10 million. In January 1975 a 14-man South African economic mission led by Foreign Minister Brand Fournie tied up a financial package including US$22 million in loans to the National Development Bank and credit lines to the army engineers' command for importing South African fertilizers and road-making equipment. The team's one visit outside Asunción was to the Department of Itapúa, the south-eastern agricultural stronghold of Paraguay's wealthy German community, most of whom settled in the country after 1945.

In August 1975, South Africa's Prime Minister John Vorster visited Paraguay with a group of top officials, most of whom later figured in the 'Muldergate' scandal: Chancellor Dr Hilgard Muller, Foreign Minister Brand Fournie and state security chief H.H. Van der Bergh. In this first official visit to South America Vorster met with all his ambassadors in the Western hemisphere in Asunción and signed additional loans to various Paraguayan government agencies. At the height of the Muldergate scandal in March 1979, the head of intelligence of the armed forces in South Africa, Major General Pieter Willen Van der Westhuizen, made a surprise trip to confer with Stroessner in Asunción. He was accompanied by what were described as his 'Paraguayan military aides', Colonel Dionisio Chaves Altumann and Colonel Victor Boettner, both Paraguayan army officers of German extraction.

Cultural and trading links between the two countries have increased rapidly, and military ties are also strong. The South African military mission in Paraguay is second only to Brazil in size and the second-in-command of the Paraguayan army, General Andrés Rodríguez, whose involvement in heroin smuggling to the USA caused a diplomatic row with the US Government in 1971, recently made a tour of South African military bases. In September 1979 the commander-in-chief of the South African armed forces, General Merindol Malan, paid a return visit to Paraguay.

The close ideological link between the two regimes was cemented recently with the inauguration of Paraguay's embassy in Pretoria. A Paraguan priest was flown there especially to bless the building. The spacious premises, which cover an area of 1,000 square metres, were a gift from the South African goverment.

Paraguay also maintained relations with Ian Smith's illegal regime in Rhodesia. The processing of Rhodesian tobacco by a Paraguayan company, *La Vencedora*, for later re-exporting to Holland, was denounced to the UN Sanctions Committee. The Paraguayan press has welcomed white Rhodesians seeking to settle in the country, such as in this editorial in *ABC Color*, Paraguay's leading daily newspaper, on 6 October 1976: 'Among the countries which could receive the Rhodesians, ours is one of the best. Physical reasons – stability; and legal reasons – laws protecting immigrants and foreign capital. All these add up to Paraguay being of interest to those Rhodesians who decide to leave their country.' Stroessner has also opened an information office in Windhoek, Namibia, for whites interested in emigrating to Paraguay.

he was handed over to the Uruguayan authorities. In August 1977 the Uruguayan police cynically issued a warrant for his arrest, although by that time he was already under detention in Uruguay; nothing has been heard of him since.

Collaboration between the repressive forces of Paraguay and Argentina intensified in August 1979 following the arrest in Asunción of two Argentinian families, Landi and Domínguez, including their children, by a combined Argentinian and Paraguayan police squad. They were taken to the police Investigations Department where they were tortured by Argentinian police. The Argentinian police even parked their own police vehicles outside the Paraguayan police headquarters for over a week, revealing Argentinian police number plates for all to see. During the time of their detention, the Paraguayan government denied knowing their whereabouts or that Argentinian police were operating inside Paraguay.

In an interview with a Brazilian newspaper in September 1979 Sabino Montanaro, the Paraguayan Minister of the Interior, stated that never in his eleven years as minister had he participated in the handover of Argentinians to Argentina, nor of Uruguayans to Uruguay, nor accepted Paraguayans from either Argentina or Uruguay. This claim was immediately contested by a Paraguayan

## Stroessner and the United States

'In the field of international affairs I do not know of any other nation which has risen more strongly than yours against the threat of communism and this is one reason why I feel especially happy to be here'.
**Richard Nixon, 4 May 1958, on arriving in Paraguay.**

Since 1954 the United States government has consistently supported the Stroessner regime, both economically and militarily. Despite tensions with the regime over heroin smuggling (1971), child prostitution (1977) and human rights violations (1978), financial support has never wavered. Official US aid up to 1970 totalled US$146 million. Increasingly, however, US aid is channelled through multilateral funding agencies in which the USA has a controlling interest. Between 1961-79 the Stroessner regime received US$311 million from the Inter-American Development Bank and a total of US$175 million from the World Bank up to 1978, of which US$39 million was in 1977-78 alone.

In return for this financial support Stroessner has been the strongest ally of the United States and the most vociferous member of the anti-communist lobby in South America. His support for US involvement in South-East Asia has extended as far as an offer, during an official visit to Washington in March 1968, to send Paraguayan troops to Vietnam. The huge US embassy in Asunción symbolizes the dependent relationship between the Stroessner regime and the US government. It is even larger than the presidential palace which is next door.

The State Department attempts to portray the US presence in Paraguay as a moderating and liberalizing influence on the regime, although there is no evidence to support this argument.

The real explanation for the unequivoal US support granted to the Stroessner regime over so many years must be sought in the general context of United States strategy for maintaining 'hemispheric security' in the South American sub-continent. The United States interest in Paraguay in particular is for military and strategic reasons, since direct US economic interests in Paraguay are small compared with US investment in neighbouring Brazil and Argentina.

Paraguay occupies a key place as a buffer state in the geo-politics of the sub-continent. Situated in the heartlands of South America, Asunción is almost equidistant from all major capital cities of the region: Santiago (Chile), La Paz (Bolivia), Brasilia (Brazil), Buenos Aires (Argentina) and Montevideo (Uruguay); all lie between 1600-2000 kilometres from Asunción. If Paraguay were to be controlled by a left-wing government, the United States would see it as a considerable threat to the areas of the Southern Cone where their investment is concentrated. Paraguay's geographical position, far more than that of Cuba, would make it ideally suited for 'exporting revolution' and acting as a base for revolutionary exiles in the sub-continent.

United States preoccupation with the military security of Paraguay is aptly demonstrated by the Selden resolution passed in the US House of Representatives in September 1965 and signed by Paraguay. The resolution authorizes the unilateral intervention of US troops on Paraguayan soil in the event of what is loosely described as the threat of 'international communism, directly or indirectly'. Over 1,000 members of the Paraguayan armed forces have been trained by the US either at their bases in the Canal Zone or in the United States itself. A large new military academy was completed in 1972 at Capiata near Asunción at an undisclosed cost financed by a US government loan.

exile, Sotero Franco, writing to the Paraguayan weekly *El Pueblo* from Switzerland:

'Myself, my wife (who is Argentinian), my brother-in-law Esteban Cabrera and Nercio Stumps were all arrested in Puerto Yguasú (Iguazú), Misiones, Argentina and handed over to the Paraguayan police in Encarnación, Paraguay on 22 January 1977. We were transferred to the Investigations Department where we spent 11 months as 'disappeared' prisoners until international organisations managed to obtain our transfer to the Emboscada prison camp from where we were later released into exile.

Marta Landi, Alejandro Logolusso, José Nell, all Argentinians and Gustavo Insaurralde and Nelson Santana, both Uruguayans were arrested in Paraguay in April 1977 and handed over on 16 August the same year to their respective governments, using military aircraft returning from Paraguay carrying the foreign delegations to Paraguay's independence day celebrations. We saw this with our own eyes, since they were all detained with us in the Investigations Department. What has the Minister to say about this?'

Collaboration also takes place with the repressive forces in Brazil. In February 1980 Dirce Mecche Giménez appealed to the Brazilian Commission for Human Rights for the release of her Paraguayan husband Remigio Giménez, detained by Brazilian police in the border town of Foz do Iguacu, Brazil in December

1978 and handed over to the Paraguayan police. Since then Giménez has been held incommunicado in the police Investigations Department in Asunción, and since March 1980 in the *Guardia de Seguridad* prison. He had lived in Brazil for 21 years as a political exile.

## Economic Transformation

At the end of the 1960s Stroessner's was in a very secure position. He enjoyed a near monopoly of political power; military dissent was dulled by the rich pickings from a massive trade in contraband scotch whisky, cigarettes, drugs and consumer goods; professional groups and trade unions were under government control to varying degrees and he had the peasant 'backing' of the traditional Colorado Party to which had adroitly hitched his star.

However, from the early 1970s, political clouds began to loom on the horizon as Brazilian influence in Paraguay increased dramatically, displacing Argentina as Paraguay's major economic partner. In 1973 work was begun on the massive Brazilian financed hydro-electric project at Itaipú on the Paraguay-Brazil border. At the same time there was a rapid influx of Brazilian colonists into Paraguay. These factors have had a decisive effect in raising both the economic growth rate and political discontent inside Paraguay.

### Itaipú

The dam site is situated on the mighty River Paraná which rises in Brazil, and passes into Argentina after forming the frontier of both countries with Paraguay for part of its length. Paraguay had long claimed sole possession to the Guairá Falls, the largest waterfalls in the world, up river from Itaipú, which provide the enormous hydro-electric potential for the dam project. However in May 1964 Brazilian troops occupied the falls and relations cooled when the Paraguayan deputy Foreign Minister was expelled from the area by Brazilian troops during a fact-finding mission. Over the next two years Brazil consolidated its position, assuming de facto control over both sides of the River Paraná surrounding the falls.

Despite growing resentment in Paraguay at Brazilian aggression, Stroessner signed the Act of Iguazú on 22 June 1966 with President Castello Branco of Brazil. The act stated that the harnessing of the enormous energy potential of the Guairá Falls would be shared in equal parts between the two countries in the form of a condominium. This joint declaration constituted a diplomatic triumph for Brazil since it signified Paraguay's implicit relinquishment of its former claim to possession of the Guairá Falls.

The Treaty of Itaipú was finally signed on 26 April 1973 between Stroessner and President Geisel of Brazil. Itaipú is the largest hydro-electric project in the world, with an installed capacity of 12,600 megawatts, six times larger than the Aswan dam. The huge dam will extend 200 kilometres up river to the Guairá Falls which will disappear under water. In all 1,400 square kilometres of land will be inundated by the dam.

Work on the project is already well on schedule and in October 1978 the whole River Paraná was diverted through a colossal manmade diversion channel so that the dam wall could be constructed. The first of 18 turbines is due to come on stream in 1983.

The rapid construction schedule is being maintained only at considerable human cost. The enormous construction site is treated as a high security zone under the control of a binational Itaipú police force. Access to the site is strictly controlled and helicopters keep the area under constant surveillance against terrorist attacks.

Information on labour conditions at Itaipú is restricted since visiting journalists are not allowed to interview or photograph any of the 25,000 labour force of whom half are Paraguayan. Safety measures are grossly inadequate. In July 1979 the director-general of Itaipú announced that 43 workers had died so far on the construction of the dam. He added that 'this number is low considering the magnitude of the project'. Most observers believe that this is a gross under-estimation of the number who have died so far. Trade union activity is banned and workers who organize against the harsh work rhythm are dismissed thanks to a network of paid informers among the labour force. Nevertheless, there have been several wildcat strikes; the largest was on 8 March 1978 when 3,000 workers rioted in protest against delays in payment of wages and poor living conditions in the company barracks.

The terms of the Itaipú treaty, which were only made public after its signing, have provided a major focus for opposition to the

Stroessner regime inside Paraguay. The main points of criticism are:

1. Paraguay has no effective control over the cost of the project, which has escalated from US$1,800 million in 1973 to a current estimate of US$12,000 million.

2. Paraguay's share of the escalating cost of the project is financed by loans from Brazil, which will be paid back largely through the sale of part or all of her 50% share of the electricity generated.

3. The price at which Paraguay will export electricity to Brazil is far below comparable international standards and is fixed for the next 50 years.

4. The bulk of the contracts for the construction of Itaipú have gone to Brazil with Paraguay obtaining only minor contracts for housing and materials provision, amounting to no more than 15% of the total.

According to the Itaipú treaty, Paraguay must inform Brazil by 1981 of the share of its own energy from Itaipú which it intends to reserve for domestic use. Key members of the ruling elite are known to be receiving bribes to ensure they continue their pro-Brazilian stance and it is likely that some if not most of Paraguay's share of the energy will be sold at a low price to Brazil and will not be used to stimulate national industry. A nationalist business group has emerged and is pressing for maximum domestic utilization of the energy through the creation of energy intensive industries such as an aluminium smelter and paper mills, and a massive programme of rural electrification. These proposals for an alternative national development strategy challenge Stroessner's hitherto unquestioned control of the country's economic policies, and is leading to a broader based and more outspoken opposition movement than ever before.

The Itaipú project has been a major factor in generating economic growth in Paraguay, but growth dominated by Brazilian and transnational companies. The project itself has attracted huge amounts of foreign investment, but it has also stimulated the gradual urbanization of the surrounding area and the rise in land values in the virgin forest lands of Alto Paraná and Itaipú. The region has been opened up for massive colonization by Brazilian nationals, who have been followed by foreign companies with large scale plans for agro-export production. Adequate roads now link the area not only to Asunción but to Paraná state in Brazil which gives Paraguay access to world markets through the Brazilian ports of Santos and Paranaguá. The population in the area has risen from 160,000 in 1972 to over 600,000 by 1980. Most of this increase is a result of Brazilian immigration.

Paraguayan nationalists believe that this 'silent invasion' is a conscious strategy promoted by the Brazilian government to provide a 'cordon sanitaire' around the Itaipú dam. This would facilitate military occupation of the area by Brazilian troops in the event of any Paraguayan government wishing to renegotiate the terms of the Itaipú treaty. Whatever the motives behind it, the Brazilian penetration of eastern Paraguay has led to considerable social and political conflict. To Paraguayan nationalists it ranks with the Itaipú treaty as a major affront to national sovereignty, while within the region itself social unrest has grown as Paraguayan peasants are being forcibly evicted from their land to make way for foreign agribusiness and Brazilian colonists.

## The Brazilian Invasion of Eastern Paraguay

The eastern border region (EBR) which includes the Departments of Alto Paraná, Canendiyu and Amambay, remained one of the few frontier zones suitable for intensive agricultural development in the southern half of Latin America, until very recently. Ever since the sales of state lands after the War of the Triple Alliance, over 60% of this enormous area of 5,400,000 hectares remained in the hands of half a dozen feudal landowners with the rest belonging to the state. Despite the high fertility of the soil, its natural resources were hardly touched, save for minor exploitation of its timber resources and some cultivation of yerba maté. The indigenous population of Mbya, Aché and Pai-Tavytera people who lived off bee-keeping and hunting without recourse to arable cultivation, were left largely unmolested.

With the fall in foreign demand for yerba maté from the 1940s and frequent restrictions placed by Argentina on Paraguayan timber exports, the EBR became a very neglected area of the national economy. The control over the land by a handful of latifundistas had continued almost unchanged since the 1880s and the population in 1962 was only 60,000, since the latifundistas carried out no colonization schemes on their land.

In the early 1960s the Stroessner government showed increasing

49

concern over spreading land conflicts between *minifundistas* and *latifundistas* in the central zone of the country around the capital, Asunción. From the 1950s, peasants working overcropped and eroded small-holdings to feed a growing population clashed increasingly with neighbouring *latifundistas* over land boundaries and communal grazing rights. Their increasing awareness of the injustice of the existing land tenure system, under which in 1956 just 195 owners held 53% of the land, was a major factor explaining the growth of the Communist Party and later the *ligas agrarias* movement in the area.

In 1963 Stroessner disbanded a previous land reform agency and created in its place a new Rural Welfare Institute (IBR). The change of name reflected the future lack of any pretence at land reform in the central zone where the economic value of the land was far higher than in any other area of rural Paraguay. The task of the IBR would be to remove squatters and other poor farmers from the central zone and dump them in fictitious agricultural 'colonies' in the EBR where they were left to fend for themselves.

The IBR has been heavily funded by the World Bank, the Inter-American Development Bank and the Food and Agricultural Organization of the United Nations (FAO). Under its head, Dr Juan Manuel Frutos, president of the World Anti-Communist League, the IBR has pursued one of the most low-cost agricultural colonization schemes ever in Latin America. Some 75% of the 600 strong staff of the IBR are employed at its headquarters in Asunción. Their main job has been to arrange transport of colonists and their families to the EBR, where they are provided with a machete, axe and hoe. On arrival in the EBR, colonists have suffered from an almost total absence of technical assistance, credit provision and state marketing channels. Nor is there any prior provision of water supply, schools or health clinics. But most important of all, colonists are only issued with provisional land titles on arrival, titles which do not constitute legal ownership. They have only seven years and a two year grace period to pay for their land in order to obtain a legal title. In the absence of legal titles, colonists cannot obtain farm credit from the National Development Bank, since it requires a land title as collateral before lending. In the absence of credit to buy machinery, most colonists have remained at the same subsistence living standard as before they left the central zone, and clearance by hand of the dense jungle has proceeded at only one hectare per year per family.

While Paraguayan settlers have had to survive with almost no government support, Brazilian immigrants have flooded into the region with support not only from their own government but from the Paraguayan government too.

Brazilian colonists began to cross the River Paraná into Paraguay in the late 1960s, taking advantage of the availability of cheap virgin land and the absence of heavy farm taxes in Paraguay. Many of them were *campesinos*, often of European origin, who were under pressure in their own country from the expansion of agricultural companies and the lack of fertile land in Paraná state. They have benefitted from a number of advantages over the Paraguayan settlers: they use rather more advanced technology, work larger farms and have access to better credit facilities, sometimes from Brazilian institutions but also from Paraguay's National Development Bank.

The Stroessner government has actively encouraged this immigration. A tarred road was built through the Alto Paraná and a bridge built across the River Paraná linking the two countries. An agrarian statute which prohibited the sale to foreigners of land lying within 150 kilometres of the national frontier was repealed in 1967.

The signing of the Itaipú treaty, setting the seal on the consolidation of Brazilian power inside Paraguay, accelerated the migratory flow, as did the sudden rise in world soya bean prices in the same year. By mid-1980 there were an estimated 350,000 Brazilians in the EBR. Today Brazilians easily outnumber Paraguayans in the area. Portuguese is the language spoken and the Brazilian *cruzeiro* is the currency in circulation. Paraguayan local government presence in the EBR is minimal and the population look to Brazil to meet their growing demand for public and social services.

Brazilian economic penetration of the region has been consolidated by the activities of Brazilian land companies, assisted by the policies of the IBR and traditional *latifundistas*. In the past ten years the IBR has sold off almost all the remaining virgin state lands of the EBR. Despite the rhetoric of its colonization programme, most of this land was not allocated to land-hungry peasants but sold at extremely low official prices to high ranking officers in the armed forces and officials of the ruling Colorado Party. In turn these speculators resold this land to Brazilian land

51

*The departments of eastern Paraguay showing the approximate area (shaded) of large-scale Brazilian colonization.*

companies at market prices which were rising rapidly as a result of the Brazilian migration and the Itaipú project. In addition, the traditional *latifundistas*, who previously dominated the economy of the region, began to sell off their immense holdings in sections to the Brazilian companies. The bulk of the land in the EBR is now in foreign, mostly Brazilian hands.

The Brazilian companies have concentrated largely on exporting timber from the region, mainly to Brazil. Before splitting up their holdings for resale, the companies strip the virgin forest of commercially valuable timber and palm-hearts. This has led to a temporary upsurge in mobile saw-milling and canning factories in the

EBR, a process which is also under Brazilian control. Despite an official ban on the export of unsawn logs, the smuggling of raw timber to Brazil for further processing has become a multimillion dollar business in recent years.

The bulk of the forest cover is razed to the ground to increase the area available for cultivation. There is no provision for maintaining forest cover in areas subject to erosion and no compulsory reafforestation programme. Already the ecology of the EBR has been greatly disturbed. The catchment area of the River Acaray, the major river which runs through the EBR, was rapidly denuded in the early 1970s. In 1977 its river bed ran dry for the first time in living memory. As a result the hydro-electric plant on the River Acaray, which previously provided Asunción with most of its electricity supply, came to a complete standstill for over two years.

The EBR also possesses some of the most suitable soil in Latin America for intensive crop production; on a flying visit to the region, World Bank president Robert McNamara heralded it as 'the future bread basket of the Southern Cone'. The immigration of Brazilian colonists and the destruction of the forest cover have led to a rapid increase in the area under cultivation: in 1976-77 alone it rose by 60%. Soya production now dominates the agricultural economy of the region. From virtually zero in the early 1970s, soya production in the EBR has risen to over 40% of national soya production in 1979. Paraguay is now the fifth largest exporter of soya in the world with an estimated production of 700,000 tons in 1980. A large part of the output is smuggled into Brazil, and the traffic, both legal and illegal, is worth at least US$500 million a year.

The Brazilians are now being followed into the region by transnational companies who have begun to recognize its potential for lucrative agribusiness. Foreign investment in Paraguay remained small until the early 1970s. It has traditionally been concentrated in the extensive exploitation of huge *latifundios* given over to cattle ranching, *yerba maté*, timber and tannin extraction. In 1978 two transnational companies, Brooke Bond Liebig of Britain and the Ogden Corporation of the USA, closed their meat packing plants in Asunción after nearly 50 years of continuous operation in the country. At the same time foreign enclaves such as tannin extraction and *yerba maté* are being rapidly run down as the *latifundios* are sold off in smaller lots to Brazilian land companies.

53

## Smuggling – The Hidden Economy

No description of the Paraguayan economy would be complete without a mention of smuggling which is institutionalized in Paraguay and so widespread that it makes accurate estimates of the size of the economy and of the foreign trade sector virtually impossible. Smuggling and the form it takes is a major explanation of the unusually unequal distribution of income in the country, since it provides a source of enormous undeclared income for the upper echelons of the armed forces, the public sector and leading members of the Colorado Party. There are four main areas of smuggling which together account for the foreign trade sector being very much greater than the official figures:

1. Large-scale smuggling of whisky and cigarettes, much of which arrives in Paraguay 'in transit' and is smuggled out again in light planes to supply the lucrative markets in the rest of the Southern Cone of Latin America. This is a multimillion dollar business tightly controlled by the top military leaders in Paraguay, although administered by a handful of local contrabandists the most important of whom are Miguel Angel Napaut, a Lebanese, and Francisco Scappini, an Italian.

2. The smuggling of agricultural produce (cattle, soya bean, tung, mint) to Brazil and the reverse flow of all kinds of consumer durables (especially cars, washing-machines and fridges) into Paraguay from Brazil. This is a rapidly expanding trade facilitated by the growing presence of Brazilian colonists inside Paraguay.

3. The 'contrabando hormiga' (petty smuggling) which is carried out between Argentina and Paraguay by poor people who carry small consignments of basic goods (flour, rice, shirts, toiletries) across the River Paraguay.

4. Drug smuggling. The heroin smuggling trade from Paraguay to the USA is believed to have ended since 1972 when Richard Nixon successfully threatened Stroessner with cutting off aid unless he stopped protecting Mafia operators using Asunción as a staging post for this traffic. However, a lucrative trade in marijuana from Paraguay has grown up to supply the growing urban market in Brazil. At the same time cocaine is smuggled across the Chaco from Bolivia in return for Bolivian petrol. Most of the cocaine is then 're-exported' by Paraguayan smugglers.

International organizations, among them the World Bank, estimate imports at least 45% higher and exports about 60% higher than official Paraguayan government figures, due to smuggling.

Instead foreign investment is being switched to agribusiness in the eastern border region mainly for production of soya bean and dairy cattle ranching. Brooke Bond Liebig bought a large area of land in eastern Paraguay in the mid-1970s. Gulf and Western, a US multinational with considerable investment in sugar plantations in Central America, has bought 60,000 hectares in Alto Paraná, its first investment in the Southern Cone of Latin America. The Florida Peach Corporation of Miami has bought 17,000 hectares in eastern Paraguay with a view to soya bean production. It is also trying to attract other US private capital to the region and has listed the reasons for investing in Paraguay in its promotional literature:

— The natural fertility of the soil is so great that we will not have to spend large large sums of money on fertility, as we do in America.

— Yields per acre are greater than the yields for soya bean produced elsewhere. Our naturally-fertilized soya beans will have a higher oil content that soya beans grown elsewhere, thus making them more valuable.

— The cost of growing in Paraguay is less than in the USA. For example: farm labour in Paraguay is 90% cheaper than farm labour in America.

— Paraguay has an unbroken history of peace and safety, along with free currency exchange and a stable economy.

— Florida Peach joins a long list of major international companies doing business in Paraguay, including McGregor, International Products, Levi, Texaco, Exxon, Shell, Coca-Cola, Firestone, Bank of America, First National City Bank, Chase Manhattan through the Bank of Asunción, United Holland Bank, Transatlantic Bank, etc.'

The IBR has thus smoothed the path for the introduction of capitalist agriculture in Paraguay, mostly under Brazilian control but with increasing penetration by transnational corporations. Its policy of refusing to expropriate existing *latifundios* and its sale of virgin state lands to corrupt politicians and military leaders, were responsible for the subsequent transfer of the major part of the EBR to Brazilian ownership within little more than a decade. At the same time, by reproducing *minifundio* living conditions and insecurity of land tenure among the Paraguayan colonists, the IBR has ensured the availability of a cheap, highly mobile and landless labour force in the region for the benefit of Brazilian landowners and foreign agribusiness. As a result the eastern border region has become a centre of landownership conflicts in which the increasingly dispossessed Paraguayan peasantry is fighting for survival.


## Land Conflict

The growing number of dispossessed peasants in the EBR are providing a major impetus to nationalist opposition to Brazilian penetration. The rapid rise in land prices in the EBR has led to the disintegration of the IBR colonization programme. As the colonists approach completion of instalment payments, which would give them full title to their land, IBR officials refuse to accept further payments. Using non-payment of instalments as a justification, colonists are then expelled from their land, whose market value is today 50 times greater than the official IBR selling price, and which is later resold by corrupt officials to Brazilian land companies, at a vast profit. Land evictions have also occurred among squatters occupying unutilized land belonging to the traditional *latifundios* which once dominated the local economy. Land sales to Brazilian companies are negotiated 'free of occupants' and squatters are forcibly removed, with the help of police and the army to make way for new agribusiness ventures and Brazilian colonization schemes.

The number of land evictions has increased dramatically since 1977 as the 'frontier' of Brazilian migration moves westward across the EBR, breaking up the IBR colonies and entering areas traditionally occupied by peasants.

Mobilization amongst Parguayan colonists and squatters in opposition to Brazilian penetration and the official encouragement behind it has increased markedly. At first, dispossessed *campesinos* travelled to Asunción en masse to present their grievances to IBR officials and to the press. Growing realization of the complicity of the IBR itself in the process of Brazilian penetration, as exposed in the press, has led to a resurgence of the *ligas agrarias* independent peasant movement in the EBR as the *campesinos* begin to fight to defend their land.

A striking example  of the growing popular resistance to land

# The Plight of the Paraguayan Indians

The indigenous population of Paraguay now numbers less than 100,000, distributed in 17 ethnic groups throughout the country. Ever since the Spanish conquest, which first dispossessed them of their lands, the Indians have been relegated to the lowest position in Paraguayan society. Despite the fact that popular Paraguayan culture extols the 'Indian heritage' and that the Guaraní language is a truly national language spoken by the bulk of the population, there is a widespread and deep prejudice against the Indian, itself the result of centuries of religious indoctrination condemning the 'heathen savage'.

The bulk of the indigenous population is already incorporated into the capitalist economy, as highly-exploited wage labour on the Mennonite farms and tannin factory of the Chaco, as peons on cattle ranches or as tourist attractions in Aunción. The plight of the minority of 'independent' Indians has worsened in recent years as the rapid destruction of the forest cover in the east and the fencing of cattle lands in the Chaco have speeded up the destruction of an indigenous culture based on the free availability of, and respect for, the land.

In 1973 anthropologist Mark Munzel denounced in the world's press the genocide of the Aché Indians of the Alto Paraná. He reported 343 cases of Aché deaths over a two year period as a result of manhunts organized by fanatical United States missionaries of the New Tribes Mission. Despite the international outcry and government assurances that manhunts had ceased, new accusations were launched in 1980 against the New Tribes Mission in Paraguay. Assisted by spotter planes, they are now organizing manhunts to capture Indians of the Ayoreo tribe, the last remaining ethnic group in the Chaco to succumb to the 'forces of civilization'.

As evictions of *campesinos* and manhunts against Indians are stepped up, there is a growing recognition among them that they face a common enemy in their fight to secure land. Traditional prejudice against the Indians is being dispelled as the *campesino* gains a new awareness of his Guaraní heritage. Understanding of the communal farming system used by the Indians has had an invigorating effect on the cooperative movement among the *ligas agrarias*. Fearing the potential catalytic effect of the Indians in awakening peasant political consciousness, the Stroessner regime has gone to great lengths to infiltrate and undermine attempts at independent political organization among Paraguayan Indian groups.

evictions in the EBR was the rebellion at Colonia Acaray, in the Department of Caaguazú in March 1980. Between 1972-74 about 160 poor families had settled there on 2,000 hectares of land with the authorization of the IBR. As construction on the nearby Itaipú hydro-electric project got underway, a large sand deposit discovered in the colony suddenly acquired commercial value as a convenient source of construction materials. In 1976 a new 'owner' to the land appeared, with a title issued by the IBR — Olga Mendoza de Ramos Giménez, the widow of a general in the Paraguayan army, who acted as a front for a group of army officers keen to develop a sand quarry in the colony.

These officers arranged for police and troops to be sent to harass the colonists into giving up their land. Cottages were burned, peasants arrested and beaten up and crops destroyed. Legal action on behalf of the colonists proved to be of no avail in stopping the harassment. In 1976 the IBR 'lost' the document which had granted them provisional title to the land and by 1979 the case came to a complete standstill when the file 'disappeared' from the IBR archive. Meanwhile the harassment was stepped up. The final straw was when hired thugs destroyed a bridge which the colonists had built to connect the area by road to the urban centres where they marketed their produce. With no means of credit and no medical services, hunger took its toll. The deaths of several small children sparked off the rebellion, which had been brewing for months.

In the early hours of 8 March 1980 colonists seized the foreman of the quarry and forced him to march with them for 17 kilometres to the main highway linking Asunción with the nearby Brazilian border. After releasing him unharmed, and armed with machetes and rifles, 30 colonists hijacked a passing tourist bus. Explaining to the passengers that they were 'farmers who have been dispossessed of our land', they drove in the direction of Asunción where they hoped to draw attention to their plight. After an hour, as they neared the town of Campo 8, a road patrol forced the bus to stop. Shots were fired and the peasants fled into the surrounding forest. The passengers were unharmed.

Immediately the armed forces launched a full-scale search-and-destroy operation to wipe out what they called the 'common delinquents'. One thousand troops were flown in by helicopter and a temporary military base was set up at a Coco-Cola bottling plant. A curfew was imposed on all towns in the area. Complete press censorship was imposed and newspapers were only allowed to publish official communiqués on the operations. Several Brazilian journalists who tried to visit the area were expelled from Paraguay.

On 10 March most of the colonists were surrounded by troops at the village of Guyrúa-gúa, while another group including Victoriano Centurión, a founder member of the *ligas agrarias* movement, managed to slip through the army dragnet. 19 colonists surrendered to the army; they were all immediately shot by firing squad and buried together in an unmarked grave near the village of San Antonio-mí, 17 kilometres from the town of Caaguazú. On 15 March the Ministry of the Interior published a curt statement that ten 'delinquents' had died in a shoot-out with the 'forces of law and order'. The communiqué did not specify where and when this alleged shoot-out had taken place.

The authorities then began a national-wide hunt for Victoriano Centurión and the few other colonists who had managed to escape. Over 300 peasants were arrested throughout Paraguay, either because they had relatives involved in the rebellion or because they were activists in the *ligas agrarias*. Blas Rodas Rojas, a *ligas agrarias* activist suspected of sympathizing with Centurión, was found stabbed to death on the outskirts of the town of Pirebebuy, in the central zone, after disappearing from his home in Caaguazú. Marcelino Casco, a 67-year old tailor and Chaco War veteran died in the police Investigations Department following his arrest in Caaguazú under suspicion of receiving a letter from Centurión.

The Bishop of Caaguazú, Monsignor Claudio Silvero, referred to the repression in his Easter message: 'The recent violent events have brought great suffering to our people. We especially lament the absence of clarity in the information. We know that there has been unjustified use of violence in the repression. Too many have died. In addition deaths have been hidden and a climate of terror reigns throughout.'

The repression also provided a pretext for the final eviction of the colonists from Colonia Acaray, thus marking the defeat of their long struggle to defend their land rights. Some 200 troops invaded the colony, which was placed under military control. All remaining adult males were arrested and removed to detention in a military camp. After being in hiding for several weeks Victoriano Centurión finally sought and was granted refuge in the Panamanian embassy in Asunción in June 1980.

# Power Game

Paraguay is currently undergoing a period of very rapid economic growth, largely as a result of the Brazilian penetration described above. During 1977-79, Paraguay notched up the highest growth rate in Latin America, averaging 9% a year in real terms. The whole style and tempo of day-to-day life is changing in Asunción, where the 'siesta' is fast disappearing and traffic jams are choking its narrow streets.

However, the economic boon is bringing few benefits to the people of Paraguay, over half of whom continue to live at a semi-subsistence level. The economy remains in the hands of a corrupt elite who have made enormous fortunes overnight through kick-backs from Itaipú contracts and the sales of state lands to foreign companies and who pursue economic policies aimed at increasing the country's dependence on external markets and foreign capital.

The huge inflow of foreign private investment in recent years has been destined for the agribusiness and construction sectors, while very little has gone into industrial development. Despite the potential for such development through the use of the energy generated by Itaipú, the regime is planning to sell most of its share of this energy at a very low price to Brazil, to aid that country's industrialization effort. Meanwhile, every encouragement is given to the expansion of agricultural production for export, most of which is controlled by Brazilian landowners and transnational companies.

For the Paraguayan peasants in the eastern border region, the Brazilian invasion and the consequent boom in agricultural production has meant only land evictions and increased repression. The unequal distribution of land which has forced at least one million Paraguayans to emigrate in the last 40 years, is now an even more acute problem. There is tragic irony in the fact that while so many Parguayans have been forced to seek a living out-side the country, the Stroessner regime has given every incentive to foreign immigration. Apart from the 350,000 Brazilians living in the EBR, there are also flourishing farming communities of Koreans and Germans, and at least 8,000 Japanese. In addition, there are 12,000 Mennonites, from Canada, Russia and Germany, who own 500,000 hectares in the Chaco.

There is considerable evidence to suggest that income distribution has become more unequal since the boom. Despite dramatic economic growth, the minimum wage has fallen in real terms by at least 30% since 1972. The offical rate of inflation is 26% but unofficial estimates suggest it is nearer 62%. Bus fares, electricity, water and telephone charges have all soared in recent years due to a combination of rampant administrative corruption and the absence of central government subsidies to state corporations. Consequently, domestic consumers pay the highest electricity tariffs in Latin America and the price of petrol from the *Refinería Paraguaya*, Latin America's last remaining privately-owned oil refinery, is among the   highest in the world. City land values have rocketed with the boom in real estate investment, producing a serious housing crisis for the urban poor.

Economic change has sparked off policital conflict on a scale not seen in Paraguay for many years. A nationalist opposition has emerged highly critical of the terms of the Itaipú treaty and calling for Paraguay's share of the energy produced to be used to promote national industry. The Brazilian invasion of eastern Paraguay has further stimulated this opposition. The economist and president of the Authentic Radical Liberal Party, Domingo Laino, has been a most outspoken and fearless critic of Brazilian penetration of the country, describing it as a practical application of the doctrine of *'fronteras vivas'* (moving frontiers) associated with the Brazilian military geopolitician Golbery de Couto e Silva. As a result he was imprisoned in 1978 and again in 1979. In April 1980 he was briefly detained on arrival in Brazil for the launching of a Brazilian edition of his book entitled *Paraguay: Frontiers and Brazilian Penetration.*

An example of the growing strength of the opposition is the formation in February 1979 of the National Accord, an agreement between the four opposition parties — the Authentic Radical Liberal Party, the Christian Democrat Party, the Febrerista Party and the Popular Colorado Movement — for joint action 'to restore democracy' in Paraguay. This National Accord has so far been confined to joint declarations and no mass movement has been mobilized to support its objectives. Partly this reflects the near impossibility of 'normal' political activity such as leafletting, fly-posting and holding public meetings while the apparatus of repression remains intact. But it also reflects the underdevelopment of the opposition parties themselves, which still function more like

### Democracy Paraguayan-Style I

Text of a press interview with President Stroessner by Brazilian journalists during the visit of President Figueiredo to Paraguay, reported in *La Tribuna*, 9/4/80.

*Q.* Will Paraguay also have a political 'opening'?
*A.* We already have a full democracy, we live in a democratic regime. Of course, some people speak in a personal capacity. In fact they don't know what they are talking about, nor in whose name they speak. Here, we have the parties recognized by the electoral board. So you see we are following the rule of law. There they are, the political parties which have representation, just as it should be.

*Q.* Does the opposition have any strength?
*A.* The Colorado Party has a lot of strength. There are some other parties which do not have its electoral pull. It is the power of the ballot box which decides things in Paraguay. Here both the rulers and the ruled are guided by the law.

*Q.* Is it true that human rights are violated in Paraguay?
*A.* Here we respect human rights. Now, those who do not respect human rights are those who try to take advantage of human rights. I refer to subversives and terrorists — they who are outside the law. Human rights are for the well-behaved people, for the workers.

*Q.* Are you considering an amnesty?
*A.* Here we do not have to consider an amnesty because there is no need for one.

*Q.* What is your opinion of MOPOCO?
*A.* We are not shutting our doors to them. They don't come because they don't want to behave in a democratic fashion.

political clubs than parties as such. The fact remains that, thanks to its near monopoly for 26 years, the Colorado Party operates the only party machine with an effective nation-wide coverage throughout Paraguay. For this reason change within the Colorado Party itself is a crucial determinant of progressive political change in Paraguay.

## Democracy Paraguayan-Style II

Extract from the testimony of Dr Amilcar Santucho, an Argentinian arrested in Paraguay in May 1975 and held, without trial, in a Paraguyan jail until his release in September 1979.

'There are two incidents which I will never forget. The first was when they killed Mario Schaerer, a young student who was wounded on arrest by the police (the newspapers said that he died in a shoot-out). When they took him to be tortured, he passed right in front of my cell each time. After the second torture session, they dragged him, hanging from the back of one of the police, already dying. As they passed, he stared at me. I suppose that he didn't know who I was. It was as if, with his look, he wanted to fix onto some 'human being'. It is impossible for me to describe everything that his look transmitted – desperation, pain, anguish, impotence. At the same time it seemed that he was saying good-bye. He died a few hours later.

The second incident was the case of Mario Arzamendia, a 68-year old newspaper deliverer of the Catholic weekly, *Sendero*, who was accused of belonging to the OPM guerrilla movement. He was cut to pieces in the torture and then thrown out onto the patio of the Investigations Department. He was left there in the open air, covered only with a blanket. From all of our cells we could hear his cries of pain. Nobody went near him – we, the prisoners, were not allowed to. He was in agony throughout the night and died at dawn.'

There are signs that such change is beginning to take place. Firstly there are growing indications of internal dissension within the ruling Colorado elite. This is reflected in the increasingly outspoken daily press, with newspapers acting as mouthpieces for divergent views within the hitherto monolithic regime. After decades of extreme censorship and spurred on by increasing competition for an expanding readership, Paraguay's own brand of investigative journalists are taking up issues which were formerly taboo, such as administrative corruption, smuggling and the violation of human rights, though they dare not attack Stroessner directly and journalists are still subject to harassment. González Delvalle, one of Paraguay's most outspoken journalists and president of the journalists union, was arrested in June 1980, and is still in prison at the time of writing.

## News That's Fit to Print

Paraguay is the least known country in South America. This is largely the result of the control of local offices of foreign press agencies by key government personnel. For instance, the head of EFE, the Spanish news agency, is one of Stroessner's closest political associates and formerly the Paraguayan ambassador in Uruguay. The censorship of telex messages sent by foreign reporters contributes to the under-reporting of important news items embarrassing to the government. A recent example was the lack of international coverage given to a major 'anti-guerilla' operation in March 1980 in Caaguazú near the Brazilian border, which resulted in the death of 20 peasants and over 200 arrests. No stories were filed by local representatives of the major international news agencies, who accepted the government censorship applied to the national press.

A rare exposure of this control was a declaration by a Brazilian journalist, Rosental Calmon Alves of *Jornal do Brasil*, who covered the visit of the Brazilian president to Paraguay in early April 1980. He stated: 'Paraguay is one of those rare countries in the world which exercises a systematic censorship of news transmitted abroad by telex. It is compulsory for every message to be typed on to ticker tape and sent first to the telex headquarters of Antelco, the state telecommunications company where the official censor operates. Only after a detailed analysis, and hours later, does the telex operator at the public cabin receive authorization to transmit the journalist's message to its destination.'

Dr Miguel Angel Bestard, sub-secretary at the Ministry of the Interior replied that: 'In Paraguay censorship does not exist. The delays referred to by the Brazilian colleagues were possibly due to technical problems at Antelco'. Anibal Fernández, Stroessner's press secretary, said in a meeting with editors from the daily press: 'All the Paraguayan press, of all shades of political opinion can vouch for the fact that there never was, never is and never will be any censorship, neither of information published in Paraguayan papers nor of press dispatches by foreign correspondents and special envoys of the foreign press. Any information to the contrary is an infamy, which not only wounds our national pride, but also the integrity of the independent local papers which are thus portrayed as if they were under some sort of pressure restricting their freedom to inform and give opinions.'

Source: *ABC Color* 7/4/80, *La Tribuna* 8/4/80, *Patria* 8/4/80.

Secondly, there are mounting expressions of dissatisfaction within the lower ranks of the Colorado Party. There was a strong nationalist tradition within the youth ranks of the party before Stroessner took it over. Stroessner's sell-out to Brazil is making it increasingly difficult for party ideologues to portray him as the latest in a long line of nationalist heroes of the past, and the dictator's authority and leadership has been undermined. Colorado student leaders now openly attack what they call the 'opportunist neo-Colorados' who have jumped on the party bandwagon since Stroessner came to power in order to make enormous fortunes out of smuggling and administrative corruption. A leading dissenter is Dr Mario Melgarejo, a young Colorado lawyer, who was imprisoned in 1979 on charges of 'incitement to mutiny'. He had provided legal advice to poor members of the Colorado Party who in three separate incidents had taken to the streets in order to protest at the abuse of power by Colorado officials. In the town of Santa Rosa, Misiones, several hundreds protested the rape in December 1978 of a young woman by the mayor and five other local officals after she had gone to the town hall to apply for a good conduct certificate. In January 1979 a hundred teenagers from the strongly pro-Colorado Republicano district of Asunción were attacked by police after marching to the city law courts with banners demanding the imprisonment of a local police chief, Sosa Cardozo, accused of killing a youth in cold blood. Melgarejo was also closely involved in a successful popular protest which resulted in the defeat in December 1979 of corrupt party bosses who had dominated Fernando de la Mora, a working class suburb of Asunción, for over ten years.

## Conclusions

Paraguay has been involved in two of the three Latin American wars since Independence. As a result of its peculiar historical formation and tragic history, Paraguayans today are intensively nationalistic. The Brazilian penetration of Paraguay, actively encouraged by the Stroessner regime, could prove to be its downfall by providing the rallying point around which opposition to the dictatorship, both inside the Colorado Party and in the National Accord, can unite in a common programme of preserving national independence in the face of external threat.

But there is another element in the power game which has yet to assert itself: the impoverished peasants and workers of Paraguay. Their discontent has only been held down by fear; year after year thousands have passed through the infamous torture chambers of the police and there is hardly a family in Paraguay which does not have a close relative who has suffered this fate. Once cracks appear in the apparatus of repression and the dictatorship begins to falter, their discontent will erupt into a major political force. However, the demands of the workers and peasants will not simply be to channel the country's new wealth into national industry, but to use that wealth for the promotion of social and economic justice and to end all forms of exploitation and oppression.

# BIBLIOGRAPHY

Amnesty International, Briefing Paper, *Paraguay*, London 1976.

Richard Arens, *The Forest Indians of Stroessner's Paraguay: Survival or Extinction,* Survival International, London 1978.

Ruben Bareiro-Saguier, 'Culture of Fear', in *Index on Censorship*, Vol 18 No 1, London 1979.

Richard Bourne, 'Alfredo Stroessner', in *Political Leaders of Latin America*, Pelican, Harmondsworth 1969.

Inter-American Commission on Human Rights, Organization of American States, *Report on the Situation of Human Rights in Paraguay*, Washington DC 1978.

Domingo Laino, *Energética en Paraguay: Fraude y Entrega*, Talleres Fototipo, Asunción 1974.

Domingo Laino, *Paraguay: De la Independencia a la Dependencia*, Ediciones Cerro Corá, Asunción 1976.

Domingo Laino, *Paraguay: Fronteras y Penetración Brasileña*, Ediciones Cerro Corá, Asunción 1977.

Domingo Laino, *Paraguay: Represión, Estafa y Anticomunismo*, Ediciones Cerro Corá, Asunción 1979.

Mark Munzel, *The Aché Indians: Genocide in Paraguay*, IWGIA, Copenhagen 1973.

Gilbert Phelps, *The Tragedy of Paraguay*, Charles Knight, London 1975.

United States House of Representatives, *Human Rights in Uruguay and Paraguay*, Hearings before the Subcommittee on International Relations, House of Representatives, 17 June, 27 & 28 July, 4 August 1976, US Government Printing Office, Washington DC 1976.

Richard Alan White, *Paraguay's Autonomous Revolution 1810-1840*, University of New Mexico Press, Albuquerque 1978.

W. Wipfler and D. Helfeld, *Mbareté: The Higher Law of Paraguay*, International League for Human Rights, New York 1980.

# APPENDIX

## The Violation of Human Rights

1. *Report on the Situation of Human Rights in Paraguay*, Inter-American Commission on Human Rights, Organization of American States, January 1978.

### Conclusions

An objective analysis of the information available to the Commission leads to the conclusion that a state of affairs exists in the Republic of Paraguay under which the majority of human rights recognized in the American Declaration of the Rights and Duties of Man, and in other similar instruments, not only are not respected in a manner in keeping with the international commitments assumed by that country, but also have become the object of a practice of constant violation.

The many denunciations received from within Paraguay itself, information compiled by international bodies that visited the country, and a great deal of other data coming from different sources, as well as the silence of the Paraguayan government in the face of the many observations and recommendations made to it over the years by the Commission, enable the latter to conclude that, under the state of siege which has been in force in Paraguay — in uninterrupted fashion — for more than 30 years, grave and numerous acts have been committed in violation of fundamental human rights, and in particular of the following:

1. **The right to life.** Well-founded bases exist to conclude that various individuals have died at the hands of the authorities under circumstances which have not been properly clarified. Moreover, cases commonly classified as disappearances, involving individuals who had been arrested by the authorities and held for indefinite periods in 'unknown' locations, may well constitute instances of violation of the right to life, although, due to lack of direct evidence, it may not be possible to establish properly their occurence.

2. **The right to security of the person.** The use of physical and psychological duress and of every form of cruelty in order to extract confessions or to intimidate and humiliate detainees is a constant and continuing practice in Paraguay, as attested to by denunciations and other information received from widely differing sources. The foregoing is also suggested by the fact that

the Paraguayan authorities impassively receive the transcriptions of such denunciations which are transmitted to them by the Commission, while allowing the time limits established for the receipt of replies to lapse, without commenting on them in any way. In addition to the above, the Commission must note that no information whatsoever has been received regarding the application of sanctions against even a single individual responsible for such inhuman treatment.

3. **The right to personal liberty.** As noted in this Report, the detentions carried out under the state of siege—that is, without any form of trial or filing of charges — number in the hundreds. Some of the individuals arbitrarily detained in this manner have spent as much as 19 years in prison without being brought to trial. Indeterminate detention without charges or trial is aggravated, in many cases, by the holding of individuals incommunicado for indefinite periods.

## 2. The Deaths of Miguel Angel Soler, Derliz Villagra and Ruben González.

**Testimony received by Amnesty International and submitted by them to the Paraguayan Supreme Court in October 1979.**

'On Saturday, 29 November 1975, the Paraguayan police discovered some organizations of the Communist Party of Paraguay which were working in the most strict secrecy. The repression which was unleashed that day against members and anyone suspected of belonging to the PCP or of collaborating with it, continued up until approximately mid-January 1976. During this time about 70 people were detained in an inhuman manner violating all the normal legal procedures, breaking into and wrecking homes, ransacking, destroying and appropriating personal belongings. Amongst the arrested were elderly people (five men between 68 and 72 years old and three women between 60 and 65), three pregnant women, approximately four entire families including children less than 6 years old and adolescents of 12 and 13 years of age. The social condition of the arrested varied: workers, peasants, students, lawyers, university professors, teachers. Some of the arrested were used by police as hostages as they were relatives of persons the police had been unable to capture. Such was the case of the sister of Victor Jacinto Flecha who was detained for 25 days. No-one was spared from brutal treatment in the police stations, ranging from blows with truncheons, punches and kicks, to torture in bathtubs of dirty water and electric shocks. Neither the elderly nor the pregnant women were saved from the torture sessions. As in the case of Musi (a baker aged 69) and Lázaro Benítez (aged 72), who were beaten about the head with big heavy truncheons of hard rubber, as also with Bogarín (aged 70), ferociously tortured by being immersed in sinks full of excrement and lashed with plaited whips which caused deep and bloody wounds all over his body; his torturers only stopped when Bogarín was on the point of death (surprisingly, he recovered and his life was saved). The pregnant women were also cruelly tortured such as Celsa Ramírez, who was

70

lashed with plaited whips and beaten with rubber truncheons on every part of her body, and Sra. Gómez, three months pregnant, who with her breasts leaning on a table was beaten on the nipples with truncheons. Miguel Angel Soler, General Secretary of the PCP, Derliz Villagra (approximately 30 years old) and Rubén Octavio González (approximately 25 years old), members of the Central Committee of the PCP died under torture in a horrible manner, inconceivable for its cruelty and sadism. Miguel Angel Soler was arrested in the house in which he was secretly living on Sunday 30 November 1975 at 16.00 hours. He was put into a car in which he found Osorio, who was Soler's assistant, and who had brought the police to his home. Soler, having been taken to the Department of Investigations, was immediately tortured. The torturers were instructed personally by the Chief of Investigations, Pastor Coronel, who was acting on precise instructions received by telephone from President Stroessner. Miguel A. Soler was tied by the feet and hands with rope and gagged to prevent him from screaming. To disguise the noises, the torturers played *guaraní* records of José Asunción Flores, at full volume. Soler was beaten with truncheons, whips and with iron bars for approximately four hours. Afterwards they began to amputate his hands and arms. While dying, Soler shouted to Pastor Coronel "criminal, murderer, dealer in white women, drug-trafficker" and spat in his face. Pastor Coronel responded by kicking him in the chest which caused heart failure. Soler had died. It was approximately 10 o'clock at night. From that moment deep silence fell over the Department of Investigations. After a while some policemen came out of a room and began to shout in alarm "he's committed suicide! he's committed suicide!" The following day a sheet appeared in the toilets completely saturated in blood and the floor was covered with coagulated blood. From the quantity of blood it could be estimated that he had haemorrhaged 4 or 5 litres. With this amount of blood it is clear that Soler underwent amputation. Ruben González was not tortured in the same place as Soler (*Departmento de Investigaciones*) but in the *Dirección de Vigilancia y Delitos*, which is in a building almost adjacent to it and where there is a bathtub which is used for tortures, not only for political prisoners but also for common criminals. Rubén González was beaten with truncheons over his whole body until there was not a square centimetre of his skin which was not bruised, and put into the bath full of water and excrement, with his hands and feet tied. After several hours of torment during which Rubén González did not once open his mouth except to swallow the excrement or to insult his torturers, he was hung upside down, by the feet, from a beam in the ceiling, whilst being beaten with iron bars until he was dead. Derliz Villagra was murdered in the *Departmento de Investigaciones*, his hands and feet tied with ropes, gagged and beaten with truncheons and iron bars until he was deceased. The beatings which Villagra received could be heard from where we prisoners were being held and it sounded as if doors were being violently slammed; one could also hear clearly the groaning smothered by the gag. All the tortures mentioned here were personally directed by Pastor Coronel and executed by Lucilo

Benítez (including the amputation to Soler). The assistants in the tortures were Officer Esteban Martínez, who specialized in practicing karate blows on the prisoners and who displayed a ferocious cruelty, the chauffeur of Pastor Coronel, the personal barman of Pastor Coronel, a brother of Pastor Coronel, an officer called Riquelme, Inspector Sapriza (sinister and terrifying, who openly makes it clear to the prisoners that he is a Nazi), Inspector Torres (who specializes in torturing women in front of their children and in taking 'written' declarations, supposedly confessions from the prisoners), Julian Evreinoff (specialist in analysing the declarations and evidence against the prisoners), Officer Belloto (well known for his sadism and ferocity in torture), Inspector Esteche (incredibly cold blooded, as are Sapriza and Torres, in finishing off the torture). The deeds presented here should be widely circulated, especially as the dictatorship denies that Soler, Villagra and González were ever arrested. *These three people have not disappeared, but they were murdered following incredible torments*, in the presence of the Chief of Investigations Pastor Coronel and following precise instructions from President Stroessner. All the torturers mentioned in this account should be judged by the international courts as extremely dangerous criminals and their crimes should be circulated throughout the world in order not to make them feel above the law. In the same way should be judged President Stroessner for being the intellectual author of these crimes, the Minister of the Interior, Montanaro, who had jurisdiction over the torturers and the Minister of Foreign Relations, Nogués, for concealing these crimes from international organizations. The institutions responsible for ensuring respect for human rights should send a mission to Paraguay to investigate the existence of graves in the *Batallón de Seguridad*, where persons who had been considered disappeared are probably buried.'

Letter published in *El Pueblo*, Asunción, 13/3/1980.

The Editor                                                    Pirané, Formosa
El Pueblo                                                          Argentina
Asunción                                                      5 March 1980

Dear Sir,

I am writing to inform you that one day in April 1976, at about 5.45 am as I was returing from a fishing trip with my son, we saw three bodies floating in the water near a small island about 4½ kilometres from the port of Villeta on the Paraguayan side of the river. The bodies were in a state of decomposition and two of them were tied by hand and foot with rope.

The authorities at Villeta were informed and went to the place. They were so surprised at finding such a macabre sight that they did not know what to do. Just as the Justice of the Peace (JP) was about to inform the police, he received a curt communication from a police officer telling him not to move from his office and to await the arrival of a special squad from Asunción.

Two high-ranking police officers later arrived and travelled to the site, accompanied by the local police chief, the river police chief and the JP. They immediately ordered burial in graves 85 centimetres deep on a small river island, to be covered with grass and bushes. The work was done by two dockers who were given 3,000 *guaraní*s (£10) each with the severe warning that they would suffer the same fate as the people they were burying if they spoke.

The JP, a young man who studied law in Asunción, entered the deaths in the corresponding book and was told by the police 'not to speak a word' about what he had seen and what they did with the bodies. The JP was surprised to recognize one of the bodies (the least decomposed, and showing signs of fractures and blows to the head an neck). It was none other than young Derlis Villagra, fair, robust, short, aged between 35-37, whom he had known during his days in the Colegio Nacional secondary school around 1953-55. In those days Derlis was a well-known student leader who stood out, with his courage and intelligence. The other bodies were presumably those of Miguel Angel Soler and Ruben González, decomposed with head and shoulders badly mutilated and with bits of rope still tied to hands and feet.

As a journalist, you will decide the best treatment to give this letter, which denounces acts which have been covered up for a long time for fear of adverse publicity, both nationally and internationally, at the disclosure of such barbarous and reugnant acts.

Signed
Fulgencio Sosa Morinigo.


### 3. The Case of Doroteo Brandel.

In 1976, peasant leader, Doroteo Brandel, denounced land evictions by soldiers working on behalf of a foreign land company. His accusations were published in the weekly paper of the opposition Authentic Liberal Radical Party, *El Radical*, whose editor was Dr Martínez Yaryes. General Carpinelli, commander of the Second Infantry Division named by Brandel brought a law suit against Yaryes for libel and slander. Brandel was abducted and 'disappeared' for over two years.

Brandel was released in July 1978. Ignoring threats from the military, he went to Asunción and denounced what had happened to the Paraguayan Human Rights Commission, thereby greatly weakening General Carpinelli's case. A few days later, on 21 August, he was waylaid by hired assassins, shot and stabbed 17 times. The following is the letter he wrote to the president of the Human Rights Commission shortly before his death, giving details of his arrest and torture.

Sra Carmen Lara Castro  Asunción
President  10 August 1978
Paraguayan Commission for Human Rights
Asunción

Dear Madam,

I am writing to denounce my arrest and imprisonment in the Second Infantry Division, as well as the plight of more than 300 families who have been kicked off their land at Carrería-i, Yhu, in the Department of Caaguazú.

In early 1974 a military post was set up in the property of the company *Hispano-Paraguaya* at Carrería-i, commanded by Lieutenant Romero of the Second Infantry Division based in Villarrica. From then onwards the threats began, to make us campesinos, 3,000 families in all, give up the 45,000 hectares which we occupied. All the facts about the case can be found in File No.1212 dated 1974, belonging to the Institute of Rural Welfare (IBR).

Given the resistance shown by the *campesinos*, the soldiers destroyed and set fire to 48 of our homes. Later, and presumably because the evictions were not being carried out fast enough, a Sergeant Colman came, whose first act was to arrest a man called Flecha from Kilometre 7 (a settlement) and bring him to the military post. Colman stood on top of him, kicked him, shaved his head with a knife and stuck him in a cell. Ramón Duarte was also arrested and had his eardrums broken from being hit with a revolover. In another case, during a fund-raising dance for the local school, Colman turned up and tried to dance with a newly-married woman. When her husband objected, Colman beat him up and made him take his clothes off in front of everybody. Another couple, victims of Colman, were promised that they would be paid compensation for improvements carried out if they gave up their land. When they were leaving, Colman started to beat up the *campesino* and his pregnant wife, knocking them both to the floor, saying, 'This is your payment'. Then he set fire to their home.

Eulalio Gómez, another *campesino* whose cottage was burned, was taken to the police station at Caaguazú and brutally beaten around the head and body, receiving so many wounds that they have still not healed to date. It would be really endless to relate all the cases of *campesinos* who were persecuted, beaten and imprisoned at this time. There were also murders, as in the case of a whole family who were killed and buried in the woods. Their relatives were forced to dig them up and exhibit their bodies so that the soldiers could make fun of them.

On 21 May 1976 Sergeants Colman and Delgado, together with Lieutenant Romero, came to my home at 12.30 at night. They knocked on the door, saying that my brother-in-law, Lucio Gamarra, had sent for me because his wife had died. When I got up in my underclothes, I was punched to the ground by a man called González dressed in civilian dress. Colman and Delgado hit me with their guns and fired them close to me. They tied my hands and took me to Eugenio Brandel's home, arrested him in a similar

74

fashion, and took us both to a football field. Here my cousin managed to escape into the woods, even though they shot after him. They took me to the office of *Hispano-Paraguaya* (the military post) and kept me there until the next day with my hands and legs tied to a stake.

At 13.30 on 22 May they took me to Caaguazú and shaved my head. The next day they took me to the Second Infantry Division and locked me up. Three days later they took me to the office to make me declare against Dr Martínez Yaryes and deny everything that happened in my cottage. Major Guanes and Sergeant Delgado were in charge of taking down my statement. I insisted that everything I has said in support of Dr Martínez Yaryes was the truth since I was a witness to all the outrages, the burning of the cottages, the arrests and abuses. On 27 May they put me up a tree and kept me there in my underclothes for 49 days. To eat they would throw me hard biscuits. I only ate when I was lucky enough to catch them with my hands. On 12 July they shaved my head again and from 9.30 am they stripped me naked and hit me with a machete. This was carried out by Major Benítez. On 13 July they hit me with swords. This lasted until the 28th, on which day they hit me with a cattle whip (made of leather braided with iron rings) ten times all over the body, tearing the flesh. At 11 pm they took me from the cell and gave me 25 strokes with the sword. Three days later they did the same thing, and so on every three days until 14 October. During four months I received about 600 lashes all over my body. This was carried out by Lieutenant Fernández.

On 16 February 1977 they shaved my head again and put me back in the cell, a tiny room with no bed, so that I had to sleep on the floor. I would eat one day and then nothing for three days. In November 1977 an Englishman called Alan Kent was imprisoned with me. He explained that they had arrested him in Caaguazú after robbing him of all his money and his passport. Kent was with me for 15 days, after which they took him to the police Investigations Department in Asunción. It was he who informed people in Europe about my situation. In December, Lieutenant Franco and Major Benítez told me they were going to take me to a public notary so that I could sign something against Dr Martínez Yaryes, and that I would be released. They told me I should state that he had paid me to declare in his favour. I let them know that I would not do that, so they locked me up again. Throughout all of 1978 they did not hit me again, but I still had to sleep on the floor of that cell (9' x 9') without any piece of furniture in it. They gave me tranquilizers to calm me down.

In December 1977, General Otelo Carpinelli came to my cell to ask me how I felt and told me that he would receive me in his office, something which in fact he never did. On 24 December Lieutenant Franco came and told me that General Carpinelli wanted to speak to me. I was left in his office for 90 minutes but no interview took place, so they took me back to the cell. In July 1978 Lieutenant Franco came and told me that I should get ready as I was going to be released. They took me to the office where they said they would release me only if I signed a statement saying that Dr Martínez Yaryes had paid me 200,000 *guaranís* to delcare in his favour in the criminal proceedings for libel and slander which General Carpinelli was bringing against him. They told me that if I did not sign, they would lock me up for two more years. I replied that I preferred to be locked up for two more years rather sign something that was not true. They offered me all kinds of help if I declared in favour of the General. I answered that there was now very little left of my former self, that I would probably not live much longer in any case, but that I wanted to do so with a clear conscience and not bring dishonour on my name and that of my family. They insisted that I sign, telling me that I would be set free and that the military would help me.

It was then that Dr Martínez sent word that it did not matter what I signed since I had already suffered too much on his behalf. So I decided to sign a 4-page declaration at the end of which they added that Martínez Yaryes had paid me not 200,000 but 300,000 *guaranís*. They thanked me very much and released me with the warning that I should not tell anyone what had happened to me during the past two years and two months of my imprisonment. I never read the declaration which I signed in the Second Infantry Division.

Signed<br>Doroteo Brandel

QUEEN MARY
COLLEGE
LIBRARY